The company director's desktop guide

Published by Thorogood Limited
12-18 Grosvenor Gardens
London SW1W 0DH.

Thorogood Limited is part of the
Hawksmere Group of Companies.

A CIP catalogue record for this book is
available from the British Library.

ISBN 1 85418 131 9 (Trade edition)
Printed in Great Britain by Ashford Colour Press.

Designed and typeset by Paul Wallis at Thorogood.

CONTENTS

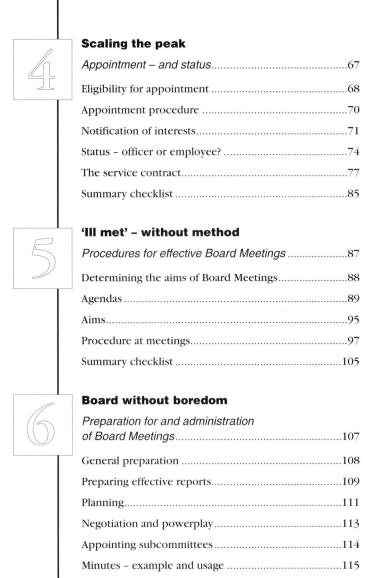

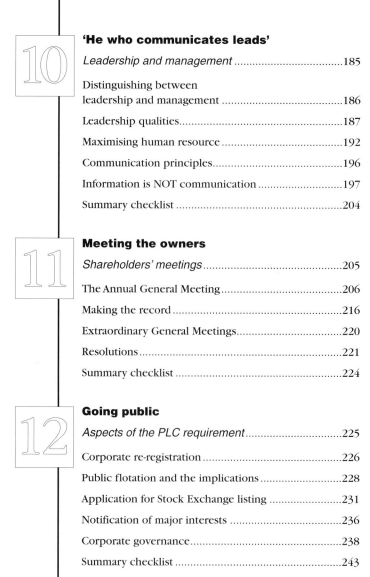

Icons

Throughout the Desktop Guide series of books you will see references and symbols in the margins. These are designed for ease of use and quick reference directing you to key features of the text. The symbols used are:

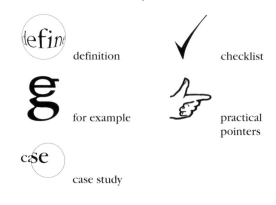

define   definition

✓   checklist

g   for example

☞   practical pointers

case   case study

Introduction

There are over 1.2 million companies registered at Companies House so there must, by definition, be at least 1.2 million Directors in the UK – in fact, since many companies have more than one Director that number is probably nearer 2 million. (On the Registrar of Companies register of Directors there are around 2.7 million names.)

Following a hostile takeover in 1985 I set up my own consultancy. As well as writing a number of books on the subject I speak each year to around 1000 company Directors and Company Secretaries at seminars and conferences. The impression is that relatively few of those holding the position have a full awareness of the obligations, responsibilities and liabilities placed upon them under Company law and which they accept with the appointment as 'Director'. The situation can only worsen as the amount and complexity of legislation increases. The maxim 'ignorance is no excuse' may be valid but with the weight of legislation placed on companies it is difficult to see how many smaller organisations can hope to remain within the law, if indeed they already are, which may be unlikely! Indeed it might be argued that that maxim can no longer apply – although to be safe it might be better to let someone else be the first to make that point in court!

Widespread lack of awareness

Assuming those attending such courses are likely to be some of those most aware of the need to keep up to date one can only wonder at the lack of awareness of the others. That these impressions are valid was borne out in early 1998 by a survey which indicated that 58 per cent of those asked were not aware of the Company Directors Disqualification Act 1986. If that were not bad enough of the 42 per cent who stated they were aware of it no less than 63 per cent felt it was not relevant to their business and 90 per cent thought it was not relevant to them personally! That Act, like all other Company Law, affects all Directors – and currently the law makes no distinction between a Director of a husband and wife business company which employs only the owners, and the massive listed PLC internationally based company employing hundreds of thousands.

Personal liability

Limited liability companies have, since the mid-1850s, operated under a system of law which has developed piecemeal and in response to scandals of the guilty few, whose actions thus visit additional requirements on the innocent and hardworking vast majority. The liability which is limited in companies is that of the shareholders – not of the Directors whose personal exposure seems to grow daily. Since the passing of the Insolvency Act 1986 (another act which experience indicates few Directors know about) Directors can be made personally liable to contribute to the assets available to creditors should their company fail and they be held to have traded wrongfully. In addition, under employment, health and safety and environmental law, Directors can nowadays be made personally liable. This worrying trend within an increasingly litigious nation shows no sign of abating – and very often such personal liabilities are not insurable.

Practical help

Currently there is a major consultation exercise under way which will, it is promised, lead to a totally new approach to Company law – and inevitably to new requirements on company Directors. With this background it seems appropriate to compile a user-friendly and practically orientated handbook to guide the layman Director through the existing maze of legislation and requirements as well as preparing him and her for the innovative law due to come into operation at the start of the next millennium.

Thus this Desktop Guide is for the vast majority of Directors who:

- Have no legal training (thus although it refers in passing to the law it is not a legal treatise)

- Need to know what they have to do (thus it is presented in an essentially practical format with checklists and hints and warnings) – are pressed for time by virtue of their other priorities (thus it concentrates on the essentials which should enable the Director to 'get by' without breaking Company law) – are concerned about their liabilities (thus it not only outlines how these can arise but also provides practical guidance on minimising the effects of these liabilities).

It would be presumptuous to seek in this book to tell the reader how to run his or her company – although there are brief sections on planning and on leadership of employees which are requirements of Directors often overlooked. Nevertheless the book tries to guide those running companies so that they can be assured they will:

- Comply with legislation

- Ensure their companies are similarly compliant and

- Minimise their exposure to personal liability.

In addition, I have included an analysis of what Directors might expect during, at least the first few years of the new millennium. Whilst to some extent this is crystal ball gazing, projecting what is happening now, to what might happen then may be less prone to error than might at first be thought.

Inevitably in a concise handbook it is impossible to explore all ramifications and obligations and thus these contents should be regarded as an essential foundation – a base for further knowledge. This law is complex and this book seeks only to act as a guide through the maze – quite properly in many instances suggesting that readers should take legal advice – however it should provide the basic knowledge that will at least enable those seeking further knowledge to ask informed questions!

David M Martin FCIS FIPD

1

chapter one

The nature of the beast

'Defining the nature of Directors and their role'

Defining the term

Memo

To: A newly appointed Director

From: The author

Subject: Your Board appointment

Congratulations on your appointment. May I be one of the first of many to wish you every success in your new role. Unlike other well-wishers, however, may I also sound a note of caution – and suggest that you make yourself fully aware of all the responsibilities you have acquired and the liabilities to which you are now exposed. You may be somewhat taken aback at the breadth of the latter – and even more so at the fact that there is very little you may be able to do about it in terms of protection. May I suggest you read on…

Memo

To: An existing Director

From: The author

Subject: Survival

As a Director of some standing I expect that you are aware of the range of responsibilities and liabilities for which you carry the can. I hope you are up to date, although since you are also responsible for running your company, the time you may have available for keeping up to date on current laws, requirements and changes may be limited. Beware – many of these changes are fundamental, and increasingly the move is action being taken against the individual rather than the corporate body. In the interests of self-protection, if nothing else, may I suggest you read on…

An appointment to the Board is a matter of achievement and praise but it is far, far more than that and those that feel that they have 'made it' when they hear those magic (and often long-awaited) words 'we'd like you to join the Board' owe it to themselves and their dependents to consider fully all the implications in at least as much detail as the perks and rewards that are now their entitlement.

Indeed, so onerous are the obligations currently placed on Directors (let alone what is to come in the forthcoming Companies Act due to hit our desks early in the next century) and so swiftly are the occasions being extended where the Director may find him or herself (purely for convenience – 'himself' and 'he' from now on) personally liable that appointees might be forgiven for feeling that the elevation may more closely resemble a poisoned chalice than a well-deserved promotion. This is not to say that any such appointment should be rejected but simply to advise that before making the jump from manager to Director, the full implications of this quantum move should be researched, understood and appreciated – which is the intent of this guide.

Joining the throng

In the United Kingdom there are over 1,200,000 companies registered at Companies House. Every company must have a Director – and most will have more than one. It is a fairly safe assumption, accepting that many holders of the office have several Directorships, that there must be in excess of 1,200,000 Directors in the UK. This is roughly 2 per cent of the whole population, which is a sizable proportion of the total, bearing in mind that more than a few of these will be wealthy and powerful individuals able to wield a disproportionate amount of influence. Because such influence and power can be exercised for bad as well as good the parameters under which Directors are required to operate are increasingly defined – and constrained. As we enter the 21st century, society is increasingly aware that power is moving away from politicians (who, whatever their faults are subject to the electorate's choice) and towards corporations. Many corporations are now wealthier and more powerful than some sizable Third World countries. As a result of amalgamations and takeovers, evident particularly since the globalisation of capital markets, the move is towards internationally based corporations becoming ever larger and more powerful. These companies and corporations are controlled in theory by their shareholders but in practice by their Directors. To many people this is a subject of some concern which has been evidenced in recent years by pressure to enact tighter controls to try to ensure compliance and responsible corporate governance. There is no doubt that this move will continue and that every Director will be required to comply with a larger range of laws, practices and requirements backed by increasingly severe fines and penalties. Indeed, even as this book was being finished we entered a consultation period regarding a complete overhaul of existing UK company legislation.

What is a 'Director'? Most people will understand or assume, that a Director 'directs' in the same way that a manager 'manages' and a supervisor 'supervises', even though they might be then hard put to actually define the verbs used to 'define' the nouns. It seems logical to require a definition of the word 'Director' and even more logical since it is Company law with which Directors must comply to refer to the latest Act to gain a definition. Immediately however we strike a problem since nowhere in Company law is the term 'Director' defined – even though the numerous obligations and requirements placed upon such persons and the penalties for their non-observance are dealt with at length. Indeed it may come as some surprise, since most companies are controlled by 'Boards of Directors' to realise that the legislation does not require companies to have a Board either – and neither does it stipulate that, if there is a Board, then it should meet. The situation is further confused by Section 285 referring to 'the acts of a Director or manager' being valid notwithstanding any defect in his appointment. By using the word 'manager' with that of 'Director' it apparently equates the role of the direction of the company with that of managing it. (One assumes the inference is that the 'manager' would be a 'general manager' rather than a departmental manager.) Although legislation is comprehensive in terms of a Director's legal duties and responsibilities it provides no guidance as to the actual role or scope of the appointee. Indeed, whilst many Directors may be aware of their legal obligations, compliance with these may actually form only a tiny part of their everyday executive duties. The Companies Act 'defines' a Director as 'any person occupying the position of a Director by whatever name called' which although it may be a warning to those acting as directors without being properly appointed that they might become personally liable, is of little assistance in terms of a definition of what a Director does. It may help if we suggest that a Director is someone who:

- **Takes complete (but possibly shared) legal responsibility for all the actions and activities of a company and those working for it**

- **Determines the aims of the company and decides methods and procedures whereby such aims are attained and**

- **Plans the activities of and leads those working for the company to achieve such plans.**

This may not be an ideal definition (and of course it has no legal standing) but at least it may serve to underline several important issues, particularly to those taking on the duties for the first time. These duties include the items listed in the checklist overleaf (which itself is illustrative rather than exhaustive).

Exposure of Directors

A Director's exposure

- Complete range of legal obligations and responsibilities. It is after all not only Company law obligations that Directors assume but also those arising from the law on employment, commerce, environment, and health and safety (all of which seem ever-increasing in breadth and depth)

- Responsibility for the actions of those employed by the company and its agents. There is an obligation to ensure, as far as possible, that they all act within the law, which in turn entails an obligation to set down and police adequate procedures and controls

- Acting as a Board, to lead the team that works for them in order to achieve the aims they have set the company, and

- To determine the aims of and for the company and generate plans to achieve such aims. Failure to attain such aims (or at least to preserve the status quo) could lead Directors into direct conflict with the shareholders who appointed them as their 'stewards' to operate their company.

The Memorandum and the Articles

Aims and purpose

Companies are brought into existence by their promoters setting out the objects for which the company was formed in a document entitled the Memorandum of Association (the Memorandum) and the manner in which the company's Directors are to operate it in a document (usually bound together with the Memorandum) entitled the Articles of Association (the Articles). On appointment, a Director should make it his first (and important) task to become conversant with the contents of both documents being in mind:

- **The Memorandum states what the company is to do**

- **The Articles state how the Directors are to do it.**

Until the implementation of the 1989 Companies Act, a company could only undertake such activities as were contained in the objects clause in their company's Memorandum. If it did carry on business not covered by the objects clause the company was said to be acting *ultra vires* (i.e. beyond its authority), the act could be void and the Directors could be held personally responsible. The 1989 Act, reflecting the European attitude to these matters, relaxed this rule stating that should a company act outside the objects clause in its Memorandum, such breach could be retrospectively ratified by the shareholders. Thus the shareholders could effectively re-write the objects clause after the act by giving their approval (which should, of course, have been obtained prior to the act). Obviously the company cannot itself carry out any acts and thus those responsible – the Directors – could be held liable for breaching the objects clause. However their liability can also be waived with the subsequent approval of the shareholders.

Historically, in order to ensure that the actions and activities of a company and its directing mind (i.e. its Board of Directors) were not inhibited by a restrictive objects clause, most company promoters would devise very lengthy objects clauses to try to cover every eventuality and avoid the possibility of the Directors acting *ultra vires*. As well as allowing retrospective approval of a breach of the Memorandum, the 1989 Companies Act introduced the concept of companies having a very simple (one line) objects clause – e.g. 'the company will be a general commercial company' which it was argued would avoid the need for such long objects clauses and the possibility of the company acting *ultra vires*. However, in attempting to raise finance for the operation of a company, most lenders will ask what business the company will be undertaking. The traditional objects clause states this, and lenders can be re-assured (at least in theory) as to the business the company would (and would not) undertake. It is reported that some lenders are wary of providing funds to companies operating under one-line objects clauses and possibly for this reason, the use of such a simplified clause has been minimal. (The document setting up the consultative process for a new Companies Act ('Company Law Reform – Modern Company Law for a competitive economy') suggests that the one-line objects clause is not used widely since it is not being seen as covering every eventuality.)

The objects clause – either detailed or simplified – gives only the most general description of the aims of the company and one of the prime considerations of every Board should be to determine its operational aims, not just for its own use as a guide in planning for and directing the company, but also as a criteria for motivating and managing those who work for it. Increasingly companies are adopting aims, visions or corporate missions in order to identify objectives and to act as a criteria for action.

Corporate aims

Corporate aims examples

Thames Trains

'Our four Strategic Business Objectives – **Run a Safe Railway, Make and Take Money, Value for Money and Service Excellence** – continued to drive all our efforts and take us closer to our vision of becoming first choice for consumers. Towards the end of the year we introduced a new Strategic Business Objective – **A Good Place to Work** – because nothing is possible without the commitment, support and hard work of Thames Trains Staff.'

BAA

'Our mission is to make BAA the most successful airport company in the world. This means:

'Always focussing on our customers needs and safety'

'Achieving continuous improvements in the costs and quality of all our processes and services',

'Enabling our employees to give of their best'.

Maynards

- To increase profit and productivity for the mutual benefit of customers, employees and shareholders

- To give complete customer satisfaction and have a proper responsibility for the community

- To provide opportunities for each employee to develop his or her capabilities

- To foster better communication between management and employees (and vice versa)

- To develop better understanding, assist decision making and encourage accountability

- To recognise the individual importance of every employee.

Duties of the Board and of individual Directors

Rolling the message out

In his book *Making it happen*, former Chief Executive of ICI and star of the BBC TV series *Troubleshooter*, Sir John Harvey-Jones states 'with the best will in the world and the best Board in the world, and the best strategic direction in the world, nothing will happen unless everyone down the line understands what they are trying to achieve and gives of their best'. Aims are for Directors to develop (ideally with the active involvement of their employees – see Chapter 10) and codify, but they need to be regularly updated – and of course to be achieved by a process of detailed planning, revision and execution of the acts entailed. Perhaps this epitomises the main role of the Director which we can summarise as '**knowing where he wants to take whatever it is that he has control of, and ensuring that the company is constantly moved towards those goals**'.

Lacking codified and promulgated aims and the plans that support them there is a danger that the company may drift into activities rather than be directed to purposeful ends – which may not be in the interests of the shareholders who appoint the Directors as their stewards. The aims also provide the shareholders with a criteria against which the performance of the Directors can be measured.

Duties

Having defined the term 'Director' and delineated the aims of the company, it may also be helpful to list the various duties a Director would be expected to perform and the manner in which they are to perform. Taking the latter aspects first, the manner in which a Director and the Board is to act will be found in the Articles which should be regarded as '**the Director's rule book**' and their contents known, if not by heart, at least in terms of a working knowledge. Like the Memorandum, the Articles are approved by the shareholders and can only be altered by the shareholders. To assist companies in drafting their Articles, each Companies Act (other than amending legislation such as the Companies Act 1989) includes a specimen set of Articles called Table A. Companies are at complete liberty to use Table A entirely as their Articles or to 'mix and match' some of the Table A clauses with their own substitutions (or to devise their own Articles). From whatever source they are drawn, the Articles belong to, and emanate from, the shareholders and are binding on the Directors.

1. Each succeeding Companies Act contains an updated Table A. Thus if a set of Articles state 'Table A applies' it is necessary to find under which Act the company was incorporated in order to find which version of Table A applies.

2. To save time when drafting, solicitors often insert in the print of the company's Articles (for example) 'Clauses 1-17 of Table A apply' and then proceed to set out clause 18 etc. Where this occurs, and bearing in mind the contents of 1 above, to avoid constant cross referencing, a complete set of Articles should be prepared, setting out the exact clauses adopted irrespective of their source.

3. With a group of companies (e.g. a holding company and several subsidiaries) it may be convenient to alter the Articles of the subsidiaries so that they all have a standard format (or are even identical) to avoid needing to remember which Articles apply to which company.

Directors could be said to have two set of duties – those placed upon them by membership of the Board and those placed on them individually. Board membership embraces the doctrine of collective responsibility – the Board takes policy decisions as an entity rather than by individual Directors (although they may also take individual decisions) and is accountable to the shareholders. It has been proposed under current draft European Company Law that the Directors of a Board could be made personally liable for the actions of each of their colleagues. Because Boards make decisions as entities it is essential that there are properly taken and approved Minutes of their deliberations and meetings (see Chapter 6) and that these are adequately protected for posterity and are available for reference.

As far as personal responsibilities are concerned, inevitably this will vary from Director to Director and indeed from company to company and the checklist (overleaf) should be customised for both company and individual. Further, in the same way that the aims need to be updated from time to time to reflect changing circumstances, so too does any list of duties. Companies do not stand still – they either expand and survive, or contract and ultimately go out of business. Further the environment, both commercial and legal, within which they operate is also constantly changing and the aims and the list of duties need to reflect such changes.

Collective and individual duties

A   *Collective*

- To ensure compliance with the Memorandum and Articles of Association of the company

- To report regularly and fully on their stewardship to the owners of the company

- To act at all times in the best interests of the company: the definition of 'best interests' can be a matter of opinion but nevertheless it is an obligation. A balance/choice may also need to be made between the short-term and long-term

  Note: As well as the interests of the company (i.e. the members or shareholders): Directors must also consider the interests of the employees (Companies Act 1985, S309), and the creditors (Insolvency Act 1986); and are responsible to customers (under various trading laws), to employees and customers, visitors and even some categories of trespassers (under the Occupiers Liability and Health and Safety legislation), and to the Environment.

- To act as a trustee in respect of the company's assets: literally as a steward for the owners of the business. Accordingly a Director must act without any additional purpose which would affect the main and overriding interests of the company (even if this means acting against his own best interests)

• To exercise the best degree of skill and care depending upon his personal knowledge and experience. A Director cannot be liable for a judgmental error but must 'give of his best' and can be judged in this respect on his level of experience. He can be penalised if he is found to have acted negligently

• To declare all and any interests and to act honestly and reasonably, particularly where his own interests may be in conflict with the interests of the company. Only if allowed by the Articles may any personal profit made by a Director by virtue of the appointment be retained. On appointment and on occurrence, when later, a Director should immediately declare an interest to the Board

Note: Failure to disclose an interest can result in substantial penalties – on summary trial to a £2000 fine, whilst on trial on indictment the fine is unlimited. In addition the court could find the Director in breach of his fiduciary duty which could in turn lead to further penalties.

• To ensure the strategy of the company is formulated, known widely and adhered to

• To formulate the aims and purposes of the company and ensure that these are both known and borne in mind internally at all times, and that at appropriate times they are promulgated, with the strategic direction of the company, externally (e.g. to the media, shareholders, advisers, etc.)

• To formulate, promulgate and ensure adherence to internal procedures, codes of ethics and required behaviour

- To ensure the company acts in accordance with the requirements of company statutes, Stock Exchange listing agreement (if a public listed company) and custom and practice for the industry

- To ensure the company acts in accordance with the requirements of all other statutes – employment law, commercial law, environment law, health and safety law, road traffic law etc.

Note: The Accounting Practices Board has recently suggested that Boards should compile a register of all the laws and regulations with which their companies are required to comply. Compiling such a register is of course merely an administrative act – the underlying purpose of the suggestion is for a complete set of the company's obligations to be generated thus encouraging compliance – and policing.

- To ensure there are adequate controls over the commitment of the company to contracts, etc., and adequate authority control over all purchases (see Chapter 8)

- To ensure the financial records and reports of the company are prepared in accordance with legal and other accounting requirements, and that such reports are filed with the requisite authorities within the required time limits and that the Auditors are given every assistance to ensure proper accounting records are being kept etc.

- To ensure the products and services of the company are developed so that continuity of earning power of the organisation is maintained

- To expand the company based on well-researched, well-prepared, well-considered, and well-implemented plans

- To ensure the continued composition of the Board with the blend of skills and expertise appropriate to the requirements of the company and its future development.

B   *Individual*

- To carry out the wishes/instructions of the Board

- To ensure all tactical decisions and actions take the same general direction as the strategy of the company (i.e. ensuring that short-term decisions do not hamper or impede the progress towards the long term strategy)

- To exercise care in all activities (see case study overleaf)

- To act honestly and provide a good example (particularly when acting as company spokesperson) promoting the corporate entity and its products/ services at all times

- To ensure the appropriate blend of skills is available at Board level (and through Board members and management) at all other levels, that all employees know what is expected of them, are motivated to perform well, and treated with respect and fairly at all times, and warned and disciplined (in accordance with pre-set rules) when performance or actions are not in accordance with requirements

- To ensure the company has formulated contingency plans to protect its earning capacity in the event of a downturn or change in demand, and the effects of possible disasters affecting operations

- To protect the corporate entity and the products/ services from criticism and attack as far as possible.

Warning – 'read before signing'

Directors are constantly required to sign a variety of documents in their official capacities. As a general rule they should always ensure their signature is described as 'Director, XYZ Ltd' or 'on behalf of XYZ Ltd', particularly when signing cheques, to avoid any possibility should the company not be able to provide funds to meet the cheque that they personally may be liable. Directors should also take care that they do at least understand the outline of documents they are asked to sign unless, for example, it is a document prepared by the company's solicitors where one would expect the Director to be able to rely on their expertise.

If unable to read all documents, it might be prudent to request that those requiring documents to be signed should make and submit a brief précis of the content of the document.

Costly 'taken as read'

In the *D'Jan of London Ltd* case, a Director signed (without reading) an insurance proposal for fire cover on a company property which included a confirmation that no Director had been previously been involved with an insolvent company. In fact the Director had previously been involved with three such companies and when, following a fire, there was a claim, the insurer, because of this false declaration, refused to meet the claim. As a result the company became insolvent and failed and the liquidator sued the Director for the loss suffered by the company.

The court held that, although the Director could be excused some liability as the mistake was 'not gross. It was the kind of thing that could happen to a busy man, although this is not enough to excuse it', nevertheless he would have to contribute £20,000 of the loss suffered since he had not shown the degree of duty of care that would be expected of him.

The judge stated that it was unrealistic to expect a Director to read everything presented to him for signature but he had to exercise some judgment; here the proposal consisted of only a few sentences.

Summary checklist

✓ Directors and officers need to understand the range of their general duties and responsibilities.

✓ Need for Directors to become conversant with the content of the Memorandum and Articles.

✓ Set detailed aims and plans for the company.

✓ Compose detailed checklist of duties of Board and of individual Directors – and ensure compliance.

✓ Arrange for preparation (and regular updating) of list of all Acts and Regulations with which the company is required to comply. List the implications and arrange compliance.

✓ Require preparation of précis or explanation of all items Directors are required to sign.

chapter two

A rose by any other name

The various types of Directors – and their responsibilities

Directors in modern corporate governance

A Director is a Director

Under Company Law there is only one 'category' of Director. Although nowhere in Company Law is the term 'Director' defined, it is generally accepted that someone who takes part in the most senior management of a company is directing its activities and is therefore a 'Director' – even if not so described (see 'Shadow Director' below) either by themselves or others.

The report of the Cadbury Committee on Corporate Governance, however, suggests that there are three main 'types' of Directors:

- Those who have executive responsibilities in the company

- Those who are appointed to the Board but have no executive responsibilities (non-executive Directors) and

- Non-executive Directors who are free from any connection (i.e. with the company and/or executive Directors) which might condition their opinions and behaviour. These are referred to as 'independent Directors' (an entirely novel concept) and the Cadbury Committee suggests the reason for considering their appointment as follows:

   'An essential quality which non-executive Directors should bring to the Board's deliberations is that of independence of judgement. We recommend that the majority of non-executives on a Board should be independent of the company. This means that apart from their Directors' fees and (any) shareholdings, they should be independent of management and free from any business or other relationship which could materially interfere with the exercise of their independent judgement.'

The concept and benefit of wholly independent non-executive Directors is perhaps one which fits the requirements of large and/or listed PLCs better than the majority of companies, but many companies of all sizes will certainly be familiar with the split between executive and non-executive Directors. It is perhaps worth noting that:

a) Much that is contained in the reports of the Cadbury Committee and its successors, the Greenbury and Hampel committees, could be replicated in Company Law (having, in Summer 1998, been subsumed into 'super code' from the recommendations of all three committees) and the current Company Law consultative document refers to the content of such codes as being 'more suitable for best practice than legislation'. However, that document goes on to refer to the need for legal enactments where matters are 'not covered by the new code, or where ... legal underpinning is necessary'.

b) Draft Company Law from the European Union suggests that there should be a majority of non-executive Directors on Boards of public limited companies. This could be a trend which will ultimately spread to, at least initially, the largest private companies.

c) The report of the Cadbury committee refers to there being a 'lead' independent Director ('a recognised senior member') and the Hampel committee report, defending this concept, insists this would not be a divisive appointment (i.e. such recognition would not conflict with the position of the Chairman).

Directors' classifications

Descriptions

It may be helpful to review the descriptions commonly given to Directors as a means of identifying the responsibilities that attach to them and any individual considerations that may also apply. Despite there being several names and descriptions in common use it must be stressed that in law there is only one 'type' of Director and, regardless of name, duties etc., all are equally liable.

1. Executive

This is a member of the Board who in addition to, or because of, his membership of the Board is authorised to carry out certain day-to-day functions including entering into contracts and managing staff and assets. This type of Director is the most numerous and perhaps the one envisaged by the parliamentary draftsmen when formulating most Company Law. Because executive Directors have a managerial role in addition to their Board responsibilities it can be difficult for some to separate their two roles and to contribute to the making of a Board decision which may adversely affect their own department or its work. Yet the need to view company problems from a holistic rather than a functional viewpoint is an essential concomitant of Board responsibilities.

2. Non-executive

The concept of the widespread appointment of non-executive Directors is relatively recent. Most company Boards consist predominantly of full-time executives. Since it can be difficult for such executives to retain an overall and objective view of the company that their duties as Directors require, in the past two decades it has become increasingly common to appoint non-executive Directors to Boards. Drawn from senior management (and often retired former Directors) from other (or even the same) industries, these Directors have no executive responsibilities, but (at least in theory) provide executive Directors with advice and input based on their experience and views unfettered by the commitment to the company and the need to earn a salary. Since they do not depend for their living on the salary drawn from so acting, they can be far more objective regarding the progress (or lack of progress) of the company, and, in essence, require answers to questions the executive Directors may least want asked.

It should also be easier for such a Director to question the legality or appropriateness of certain actions. For example, in the Guinness affair the 'wrongdoing' of certain of the executive Directors, was eventually challenged by the non-executive Directors. Should actions complained of continue, at least in theory, non-executive Directors should find it easier than executive Directors to resign in protest, the potential attendant publicity being their greatest weapon to try and effect changes.

But, of course, it is not only wrongdoing that a non-executive should be able to question. It is all too easy for executive Directors – particularly Chairman and Managing Directors – since they operate in a rarefied world of power to develop an over-confidence and belief that everything they do and feel is right. It may be – but on occasions it does no harm, and could save the shareholders considerable value, if a preferred course of action is at least questioned by an impartial observer. Nowhere is this more necessary that when a takeover is under consideration. Research indicates that shareholders in acquisitive companies rarely benefit from takeovers.

'There have now been a series of academic studies done in both the USA and Britain which show a remarkably similar pattern. By and large the shareholders of the target DO receive more money for their shares than they paid for them. But what is truly astonishing is that the shareholders of the pursuing corporations rarely see any gain in their share prices as a result of a takeover' (from *Takeovers*). A truly independent view from a non-executive may at least encourage the executive Directors to pause and reconsider.

Non-executive Directors rank equally with (and have the same responsibilities as) other Directors in all respects. The Institute of Directors and the Stock Exchange are very much in favour of the extension of the non-executive Director concept not least as it can also encourage an awareness of the responsibilities borne by Directors which must outweigh personal considerations.

Objectivity *v* subjectivity

The company had been formed to produce pine furniture just before the onset of the UK recession. To provide working capital, the three executive Directors mortgaged their homes to the bank. A year after commencement of business two non-executive Directors were recruited. They introduced some much-needed new capital but it swiftly became apparent that a major injection of capital was needed if the company was to survive in the intensely difficult trading conditions in which it now found itself. This proved impossible and, after several months attempting to refinance and/or attract new capital, during which further losses were incurred, the non-executive Directors felt that the only course of action in order to protect the creditors was to ask the bank to appoint an administrative receiver. The executive Directors, who understandably feared losing their homes, resisted this suggestion until one of them, realising the deepening crisis and the potential liability for wrongful trading (see Chapter 3) voted with the non-executives. It was later discovered that the opinion of the receivers was that when the company was put into receivership it had already passed the point when it was trading wrongfully. Had it not been for the objective viewpoint of the non-executives, the losses suffered by the creditors could have been worse and all the Directors could have been personally liable for far more than the value of the executive Directors' homes.

. . . .

3. Chairman

As previously noted, there is no legal requirement for companies to have a Board and many, particularly smaller companies, operate virtually without one – or at least without one operating with a degree of formality. There is no obligation on Directors to hold a Board Meeting in order to conduct the company's business – it can be conducted at any time. If important decisions are taken informally, it might be wise to confirm such actions at a subsequent meeting and have the decision confirmed by the whole Board (and evidenced by being minuted) bearing in mind the doctrine of collective responsibility.

Where there is a Board it is unlikely that it can operate unless one member takes the lead and acts as Chairman. Thus the Chairman will usually be a member, executive or non-executive, of the Board elected to chair the meeting of the Directors by the members. Increasingly as companies are featured on the news (rather than financial) pages of national press and other media, such chairmen can attain a high profile and tend to be referred to as 'Company Chairman'. This is a misnomer as no such position exists (although Table A states that if the Directors have elected a Chairman then he will take the chair at shareholders meetings). Further, although Chairmen tend to remain in such a 'position' for some time they are in fact only elected by their peers 'for the time being' and there is nothing to stop different Directors taking the chair at each meeting of the Board.

4. Managing Director

This position is sometimes alternatively known as Chief Executive or Chief Executive Officer – a term imported from the USA – although neither of these descriptions are currently recognised by UK Company Law and the Articles should be referred to for any titles required to be used. In many organisations the functions of Chairman and Managing Director are vested in one person. There has been considerable criticism of this practice in the past, critics inferring that the concentration of power in one person's hands can be detrimental to the overall control of the company and can lead to despotism. However, research seems to suggest that the retention of the twin powers in the hands of one person who drives the company forward tends to improve the company' performance more swiftly, compared to those where the functions are split.

Where there is a separate Managing Director function, it is more usual for the Chairman to be non-executive and to retain a policy control function leaving the Managing Director to ensure all remaining duties and responsibilities of the Board are effected. Thus the Chairman could be said to looking outwards, interfacing with external parties, leaving the Managing Director to ensure other Board members and management who report to him carry out the requirements of the Board and their own responsibilities – that is essentially an internal role. However, it is difficult to be precise about this since companies tend to operate in different ways – even, in some, letting the Managing Director assume a greater external role, whilst the Chairman adopts a lower profile. To a certain extent this is inevitable since the personalities and talents of the persons themselves may well affect the interpretation and scope of the roles.

The rights and duties of the Managing Director will normally be set out in the Articles and may be different to those of every other Director. Further, provision relating to his re-election should be checked carefully. For example under most Articles, a proportion (often a third) of the Directors are required to retire at each Annual General Meeting of the shareholders and (if entitled) are able to seek re-election by those shareholders at that meeting. A Managing Director, however, is usually excluded from this requirement although he may be counted for the purposes of deciding the number of Directors who need to retire by rotation.

5. *Alternate Directors*

Such appointees act as a kind of proxy for their principal for whom they are the alternate and have right to receive all matters sent to their principal. Alternates can only be appointed if the Articles allow and with the agreement of the Board. If an alternate's principal attends a meeting then the alternate cannot also attend but he can attend (which is the purpose of the arrangement) if the principal cannot. The appointment and recording and filing of details is identical for both alternate and principal – as are their rights and duties.

6. Nominee Directors

These are sometimes appointed by (for example) a major shareholder who wishes to exercise some control over the Board and company. (In fact care should be taken if exercising control in this way as it can have the effect of making the shareholder a shadow Director – see below.) Nominee Directors owe obligations to two separate bodies and may need to take care to avoid conflicts of interests. A nominee Director may have enhanced voting rights (e.g. a vote exercised by one or more nominee(s) may rank greater than the combined votes of all other members). If the nominee is appointed by another company and has enhanced (i.e. controlling) voting rights, then the company may be regarded as being a subsidiary of the appointing company, with all the implications that such a relationship entails.

7. Shadow Directors

The concept of a person exercising control over a Board as a kind of 'eminence grise' or shadowy manipulator was introduced by Companies Act 1985. That Act stated that all persons 'in accordance with whose instructions the Directors are accustomed to act' become shadow Directors. Thus, a major shareholder or a creditor owed a considerable sum, who regularly gives instructions to the Board with which the Board complies, could be regarded as a shadow Director. Similarly representatives of the management of a parent company who regularly instruct Boards of their subsidiaries in such a way so that the Board of the subsidiary follows their instructions could also be regarded as shadow Directors. The danger for shadow Directors is that, should the company fail and be held to have traded wrongfully they could be required to contribute from their personal assets for the benefit of the creditors – just as can the other Directors. To protect parent company executives in such a situation, the parent company should be made a Director of the subsidiary. In that event the executives simply act on behalf of the parent company as Director.

Of course if the company fails and is held to have traded wrongfully the parent might then be required to contribute to the creditors' losses. The possibility of the company failing might have been the reason for forming it as a subsidiary (i.e. if it fails only the assets held within the subsidiary are lost) in the first place and this process would then negate the aim of the parent company not being responsible for losses incurred by their subsidiaries.

'Shadow Directors' are legally Directors and their details must be retained by the company and filed with the Registrar. The problem the person responsible for filing may experience in trying to file details of a shadow Director is the latter's refusal to sign the 'consent to act' certificate on the form because they do not want their 'shadowy' status to gain such recognition. In such a case legal advice should be taken, as the Registrar will not accept a notification of a Director's appointment unless the consent to act form is signed.

Further classifications

  a) Associate, local, divisional etc., Directors. If allowed by its Articles a company may be able to grant to an employee, the rank of 'Director' qualified by descriptions such as those set out above, to indicate that the person has been granted authority at such a level. Such appointees are rarely Directors in the legal sense (i.e. recognised under Company Law) and they should not use the title in such a way that it suggests that they are. This is more for their own protection than the companies as once again they could unwittingly assume liabilities in respect of decisions to which they were not a party.

  b) Titles such as 'Director of ....'. Although some companies use such a description for executive Directors, this style may also be used to grant a level of authority to a person who is not a Board member and may not even be an employee. There is a danger here for the person using such a description since they could be deemed to be holding themselves out as a Director. In that event, they could find themselves sharing in the responsibilities and liabilities of a Director without necessarily having any say in the Board decisions impacting such responsibilities. Should the company fail, and the Directors be held to have traded wrongfully, they could also be liable to contribute to the assets available to the creditors.

Directors' duties

All Directors are regarded as having three duties: A duty of care, a fiduciary duty and a duty to act within their powers.

The duty of care

Until recently the duty of care required of a Director was not thought to be too onerous. However, the ruling in the following case study indicated very clearly that this was not so.

Detailed attention required

In *Dorchester Finance Co Ltd & anor. v Stebbing and ors* there were three Directors of the company of whom two, X and Y, were effectively non-executive and left the running of the company to Z. X and Y often signed blank cheques for use by Z, and made no enquiry of how funds were obtained or used. The court found that both X and Y had failed to apply the necessary skill and care in the performance of their duties (and indeed that they had failed to perform any duties in their positions as Directors). In addition Z (who, like X was a qualified accountant) had failed to exercise any skill or care as a Director and had misapplied the assets. All three Directors were held to be liable for damages.

In the judgement the court ruled:

- Each Director must exercise in his duties the degree of skill that may reasonably be expected from a person of his knowledge and experience

    Note: In considering liability in wrongful trading – see below – a court might consider a Director who is a qualified accountant to be more culpable than a (say) personnel Director, because of the former's professional training and knowledge in the corporate field.

- A Director must in the exercise of his duties take such care that a man might be expected to take on his own account

    Note: The question that could be asked is 'Would I be so cavalier concerning these funds, were they my own rather than those of my company?'

- A Director must exercise the powers granted to him in good faith and in the interests of the company of which he is a Director

WARNING: This ruling demonstrates that in terms of liability there is no distinction between non-executive and executive Directors' responsibilities.

The fiduciary duty

'Fiduciary' can be roughly translated as requiring 'good faith'. Thus, under this duty the Director must act in good faith in terms of what he considers the best interests of his company – if necessary even sublimating his own interests where these conflict with the company's best interests. This does not mean that if an outsider feels the best interests of the company would require different actions, the Directors are necessarily wrong. It is the belief of the Directors that must be examined – so long as it is reasonable for them to have such a belief then that is acceptable. The court will not interfere unless it can be shown that no reasonable Director could have held such a view.

The great difficulty is that Directors owe duties to various interested parties, particularly:

- To the shareholders (via Company Law)

- To their employees (via Company and Employment Law)

- To the creditors (via the Insolvency Act)

- And even to the environment

and it may be difficult to act in good faith in respect of one party without adversely affecting the interests of another. To provide some relief to those caught in such a conflict, section 727 of the Companies Act 1985 stipulates that if a Director has acted 'honestly and reasonably' he can be excused any negligence or breach of duty etc.

Putting company interests before one's own interest emphasises the need for Directors to declare matters in which they have interests which might conflict with those of the company. The Articles should be referred to for guidance, or, if they are silent, legal advice taken, to ensure compliance regarding speaking, voting etc. on such matters.

1. Simply because a benefit might or could accrue to the Director would not necessarily mean that pursuing it could be a breach of the fiduciary duty since in some instances the interests of company and individual could coincide – or at least may not conflict.

2. Failing to disclose an interest in business or a matter involving the company can result in the Director receiving a personal fine of £2,000 or on trial on

indictment an unlimited fine and potential further action for breach of fiduciary duty.

3. The company is prohibited from altering its Articles or including a term in a Director's contract which seeks to absolve or indemnify Director from liability for negligence, breach of duty or trust.

The duty to act within powers

The powers of the company are set out in the Memorandum and the way the Directors are required to act in the Articles. Directors have an obligation to ensure their company does not exceed such powers (Lord Denning referred to the Directors being the 'mind' directing the 'body' that is the company.) In fact, as noted in Chapter 1, since the passing of Companies Act 1989, it is now possible should a company exceed the powers in the Memorandum – i.e. to be acting *ultra vires* – for it to obtain retrospective approval for the act from the shareholders. In such circumstances not only should the shareholders be asked to ratify the act that was *ultra vires* they should also be asked to absolve the Directors for liability resulting from the breach. If the shareholders do not absolve the Directors then the latter can be held personally liable for the breach. The powers of the Directors are set out in the Articles and should a Director act in breach of the requirements then he could be held personally liable for the breach. Once again the shareholders could be asked to ratify the breach subsequently (or to approve the Director exceeding the Articles prior to this happening).

In each case should the shareholders ratify the exceeding of powers either in the Memorandum or Articles the resolution approving this must be filed with the Registrar as the effect is to alter these documents of record.

Duty to file information

Regardless of the nomenclature of those appointed by the shareholders (or by the Board subject to shareholder ratification at the next following AGM) or of those acting as Directors (i.e. any persons holding themselves out to be Directors) all have a full legal responsibility for the company as a legal person and all its actions, and those of its employees etc.

To take up the appointment, personal details of each Director must be provided to the company which must record it and file it with the Registrar of Companies. This is just a small part of the information that limited companies are required to file with the Registrar and one of the legal obligations placed on Directors is to ensure that such information is filed within the required time limits which are increasingly backed by the imposition of fines.

Each year all Directors are obliged to ensure that the company files:

- The report of the Directors

- The accounts for the latest financial period

- A balance sheet as at the end of that period – an annual return confirming details of the Directors, share capital, shareholders, etc.

This obligation to disclose and file information can be regarded as the 'price of limited liability protection'. With their limited liability protection the shareholders can never be asked to contribute more than the amount they paid for their shares to satisfy the debts due to the company's creditors. So that the latter know – at least in theory – the state of the liquidity of the company with whom they are dealing, or are contemplating dealing, the company must file this information which is then regarded, since it is filed with, and can be displayed to, everyone at Companies House, as being in the public domain. Of course in practice the shareholders' investment (i.e. the share capital) may actually be the smallest part of the assets available to the creditors. Filing is an ongoing liability and although it is usually delegated to the Company Secretary, it remains the Directors' responsibility to ensure filing takes place. Indeed, a repeated filing breach can entail disqualification from acting as a Director.

Summary checklist

✓ Directors must be, and keep aware of, general developments in Company Law and corporate governance requirements.

✓ Directors should be appointed to the positions/descriptions, and in accordance with the requirements laid down in the Articles.

✓ Understand the three types of duty expected of a Director – and comply therewith.

✓ Ensure filing with Registrar is kept up to date.

chapter three

Board members – and others – beware

Liabilities and protections

Range of legislation affecting companies

Our litigious society

In the UK we live – and members of Boards must direct and operate their companies – in an increasingly litigious society, one which seems to be reflecting a trend in the USA where there are more lawyers per head of population than anywhere else in the world. Similarly those responsible for the wealth-creating entities of our society are being made more accountable for their actions – and liable for non-compliance. As companies grow in size and power, governments are seeking to impose more controls on them and their activities – and on the activities and scope of control of those that direct them. Whereas once a Director needed only to have knowledge of and to consider the implications of Company Law to check his responsibilities, nowadays he needs to appreciate the implications of:

- A vastly increased (and increasing) number of commercial laws not least those protecting consumers and customers

- The whole gamut of employment law (which itself is increasing and developing and in the event creating situations where what is required is actually unclear) including all the anti-discriminatory legislation

- Environmental considerations, which are likely to expand swiftly

- Health and safety law

and so on.

His task is not made any easier by the fact that some Company Law obligations do not appear in company legislation but are included in Acts related to general matters (for example see the impact of the Criminal Justice and Theft Acts in the checklist opposite).

Despite their best endeavours, it is difficult to imagine that there are many companies which act legally throughout their life. The fact that very often such breaches will be related more to ignorance than intent is, ignorance of the law being no defence, of little comfort since the breach could still render individuals liable. In the checklist below are set out the major Acts related to a Director's Company Law obligations.

Company legislation résumé

1.   'Companies Act 2001'

Currently a consultative exercise is taking place which will eventually lead to a new Companies Act in the early years of the 21st century. It is claimed that this Act will be very different in approach, scope and presentation to previous Acts which have simply tended to react to situations and to amend previous legislation.

Note: There has been a suggestion that the require-ments of PLC and LTD companies will be separated and the obligations on the latter alleviated. Currently Company Law makes very little real distinction (in terms of obligations) between the two types of companies.

2.   Companies Act 1985

There have been many Companies Acts. The latest, the 1989 Act largely amends the last definitive Act – the 85 Act. Although there was (and is, since some items have still not been implemented) new law in the 89 Act, it does not stand on its own but mainly updates legislation by amendment of existing statute.

3.   Companies Act 1989

Amends the Companies Act 1985 in a number of ways particularly reflecting the requirements of European legislation.

In referring to the 'Companies Act' care should be taken to use a version of Companies Act 1985 which has been updated by the 89 Act amendments. There are still a number of amendments (e.g. the rules regarding the notification of charges over company property) which have yet to be introduced.

4. Business Names Act 1985

Deals with requirements placed on companies to advertise certain salient details about themselves wherever they trade.

5. Criminal Justice Act 1993

Restricts and controls spread of confidential information to those who by using it may be able to gain value buying or selling shares (i.e. insider dealing – see Chapter 9). Such information is termed 'price sensitive' – since open knowledge could affect the price quoted on the Stock Exchange.

6. Company Directors' Disqualification Act 1986

Sets out events that could bring about the disqualification, etc., of Directors as well as penalties and sanctions (e.g. failure to file information etc.).

WARNING: Some idea of the general ignorance of many Directors of their obligations can be gained by the results of a survey referred to by the Institute of Directors in March 1998. 58 per cent of Directors asked were not aware of this Act even though its penalties include preventing them continuing to act as Directors. Of the 42 per cent who were aware of the Act, 63 per cent felt it was not relevant to their business and 90 per cent thought it was not relevant to them personally! The Act covers all Directors of all companies.

7. Company and Business Names Regulations 1981

Provides for disclosure of names and controls the use of a list of names without authority of their controlling bodies.

8. Public Companies (Disclosure of Interest in shares) Regulations 1988

Defines 'interests' in shares in public companies that must be disclosed.

9. Companies (Registers and other Records) Regulations 1985

Grants rights of access to company records for a range of interested persons (see Chapter 8).

10. Companies (Disclosure of Directors' Interests) Regulations 1985

Alleviates the rules regarding the disclosure of interests in the shares of their companies by Directors, by excluding certain categories of interest.

11. Companies (Forms) Regulations 1985 (and amending regs. 1987)

Specifies the content and administration of certain forms required to be filed under the Companies Act. This grants the Registrar of Companies powers to vary the type and manner of submission of the various company forms and returns.

As a result of these regulations the Registrar is constantly updating and revising such forms and care should be taken to ensure the latest version is being used to avoid an out-of-date form being rejected and any replacement failing to meet the correct filing date.

12. Oversea Companies (Accounts) Order 1990

Sets up controls regarding the filing times for the submission of accounts for overseas companies.

13. Companies (Summary Financial Statements) Regulations 1990

Grants authority to companies to send to their shareholders, summary statements in place of the full accounts and report, provided the shareholders give permission first (see Chapter 13).

14 Companies (Single Member Private Limited Companies) Regulations 1992

Enacts the EC directive requiring there to be a means whereby a single shareholder could set up/control a limited company. Previously all companies had to have at least two shareholders and if a shareholder remained a sole shareholder for more than six months he could be held personally liable for the debts of the company.

15. Insolvency Act 1986

Regulates the operation of companies by outlawing wrongful and fraudulent trading and setting penalties for offenders, including requiring a personal contribution to a shortfall of assets in the event of a liquidation (see below).

16. Theft Act 1968

Deals with fraud offences in general and with the liability of company officers for offences committed by the company and for false statements made by company Directors in particular.

The liability range

The Acts set out in the above checklist cover a Director's major duties and responsibilities in terms of Company Law. But these are only a small part of the whole and the detail and decisions of cases that follow should help place the matter in perspective.

Personal liability for signing documents

Directors can be held liable for the effect of statements to which they append their signature and thus they should take care to read or have knowledge of the contents of documents that they sign. See the D'Jan case featured in Chapter 1 and the *Dorchester Finance Co Ltd & anor v Stebbing & ors* in Chapter 2.

Safety obligations

1. Motor accident

A coroner held that a company's management was grossly negligent in allowing a lorry to operate even though none of its brakes were working. The lorry ran out of control and killed six people. Two Directors of the company faced charges related to unlawful killing under the Road Traffic Act. Eventually the company that operated the lorry were fined £5,000. Originally personal charges against the Managing Director and transport manager were brought, although these were withdrawn once the company pleaded guilty.

2. Accident at sea

In the Lyme Bay canoe tragedy case (where several young people taking part in an open sea canoeing experience drowned) both company and Director were found guilty of manslaughter – the Director was jailed for three years whilst the company was fined £60,000.

3.   Building site accident

In Germany, an English property developer was prosecuted following the death of a bricklayer who fell from a building being erected in the eastern part of the country. The developer was given a five month prison sentence (suspended), fined £6,500 in respect of negligent manslaughter and ordered to pay the bricklayer's widow a further £4,500.

Under current proposals, fines that could be levied are unlimited, compensation could also be ordered to be paid to the families of victims (as occurred in the German case referred to above, and imprisonment of the culpable is envisaged).

4.   Illegal employment of children

In a case brought by the Health and Safety Executive, a company was fined £2,000, a Director £4,500 and a manager £7,500 for employing under-age children for long hours.

Employment obligations

1.   Employees discrimination
    against another employee

If employees (including Directors) discriminate against, or harass or victimise other employees, in a situation where the company has laid down rules regarding acceptable behaviour and has drawn the rules to the attention of the employee and regularly polices such rules, the employees may find that they are either joined in an action with their employer or action is taken against them individually. If the company fails to lay down rules, or having laid them down fails to police them, or 'turns a blind eye' when advised of the matter, then it could find it is liable even though the act was committed by an employee.

2. Costly careless words

In the *Bryans v Northumberland College of Arts & Technology* case, a total of £29,900 was awarded to Mr Bryans whom, amongst other things, had been called 'an Irish prat'. Of the total, although the College had to pay £13,000, his line manager had to pay £6,500, the curriculum Director £1,500 and the colleague who actually said the words £5,000. The awards were required to be paid by the individuals themselves.

In the *Enterprise Glass Co Ltd v Miles* case the Employment Appeals Tribunal ordered a male employee who had sexually harassed a female employee to pay her £750 compensation. It also ordered the company to pay her £1,000, the company having been held not to have provided a working environment in which the employee could work at ease.

3. Bullying and harassment

In the *Jones v Tower Boot* case the Court of Appeal has held that the company was responsible for employees who branded, taunted and severely harassed a young black employee.

Under the Criminal Justice Act 1994, harassment is now a criminal offence punishable by a fine of up to £5,000 and/or imprisonment of up to six months. Under the Protection from Harassment Act 1997 aggravated harassment is subject to up to five years imprisonment and/or an unlimited fine. It might be worth referring to this in internal guidance documents.

Commercial requirements

1. Water pollution

In the *National Rivers Authority v Alfred McAlpine Homes East Ltd* case, a company was held liable for pollution caused by subcontractors washing cement into a stream.

The court regarded the people responsible for directly causing the pollution as acting within the course and scope of their work.

2.   Breach of regulations

In a long-running court case regarding the supply of ready mixed concrete a company stated that it tried to ensure at all times that their employees complied with the law and trading guidelines. Whilst the Court of Appeal held that the company could not be liable for the action of its employees when they wilfully broke such rules and regulations and disobeyed instructions, this ruling was overturned by the House of Lords which held that a company WAS liable for the acts of its employees (even though the company had forbidden such acts). The House of Lords also commented that the original fines imposed (of £25,000) were too low.

3.   Environmental matters

Officers of companies are personally liable for damage to the ozone layer caused by harmful emissions into the atmosphere generated by their companies' activities.

Liability protection

With this array of potential liabilities an understandable question is 'how can I eradicate my exposure?' and the only truthful answer is that you probably can't! However it may be possible to at least minimise it – and/or alleviate its impact by considering two approaches which we can entitle risk management and risk transference.

Risk management

In this context risk management encompasses the need to ensure that there are procedures for dealing with the various aspects of business that could give rise to claims.

The content of such procedures is outside the scope of this book (although comprehensive suggestions appear in other manuals written by the author) but it is essential that such procedures address the following principles:

Principles for internal procedures

Procedures must:

1. Address the particular problems (such as those set out above) which could create liability claims for the particular company.

2. Be regularly updated to reflect changes in law and the attitudes to laws (for example, the impact of Tribunal decisions in employment law matters can have the effect of changing, if not the law, at least its previously understood implications or interpretations which unfortunately has the effect of making understanding the requirements very difficult).

3. Be phrased in user-friendly language in order that comprehension by all is attained.

4. Be promulgated comprehensively with everyone reminded of the implications and requirements (and particularly of any changes thereto).

5. Be policed rigorously and regularly so that everyone understands that the required code of conduct must be adhered to at all times.

In particular Boards should ensure that employees are aware of the requirements placed upon them to comply with procedures etc. (Note: the requirements set out in Chapter 8 could also be incorporated here.)

Thus, taking the rapidly increasing incidence of discrimination claims, if there is a Dignity at Work or Equal Opportunities policy which, *inter alia*, requires all employees to treat others with respect and this policy is regularly brought to everyone's notice, and breaches are dealt with promptly and with appropriate severity, then it may be possible for the company and/or its officers to be absolved from liability in the event of an employee breaching the policy. Conversely the absence of such a policy places the employer at an immediate disadvantage.

The development of policies such as is suggested here is not simply a question of prudent defence against liability claims, as shareholders, who ultimately bear the cost of such claims by diminution of their funds could argue that failure to devise and implement such policies is a breach of a Director's duties.

Nowhere is this more clearly demonstrated that in the current attitude to companies which do not take appropriate action to deal effectively with the computer 'millennium bug'. If the business is damaged because the company's computers fail on 1st January 2000, it is at least arguable that the shareholders could hold the Directors liable.

Risk transference

Risk transference entails an acceptance that there may be risks but that someone else should bear the cost. Whilst in some cases this may be possible there are several important principles to bear in mind which are set out in the checklist below.

Limiting protection

a) As already noted a company cannot alter its articles or include a term in a Director's contract to absolve or indemnify him from liability for negligence, breach of duty or trust.

b) Many of the instances where a breach of law incurs liability now entail a criminal as well as a civil penalty, but it is impossible to insure against such actions (since it is against the public interest to insure against a criminal act) – and would be improper (and almost certainly *ultra vires* its Memorandum) for a company to grant such an indemnity in such circumstances. For example, in an action for Wrongful Trading, a Director found guilty would almost certainly be found to have acted dishonestly so no claim would be entertained by the insurer.

c) The acts required of a Director are those allowed by the Articles and if a Director acts outside the requirements of its Articles the company could not without the shareholders' agreement indemnify such acts. Thus actions brought for negligence, breach of trust or breach of duty could not be subject to an indemnity issued by the company unless they were successfully defended.

However, the Companies Act 1989 amended the Companies Act 1985 by granting companies the right to effect Directors' and Officers' Liability Insurance cover. Further, provided the cost is declared in the Directors' Report in the Annual Report, then the cost of the premiums in respect of such a policy can be met by the company. Recent amendments to Finance Acts have also prevented the Inland Revenue from regarding the premiums paid as a benefit in kind for those Directors and others covered by it.

Some authorities have queried whether, since such a policy is to cover the Directors, they can approve such a benefit, as each will have an interest in the item of business and thus there may not be a disinterested quorum present at the meeting.

In case this is arguable it may be preferable either to amend the Articles to grant the Board the right to take out such a policy or to effect at least two policies - each covering some of the Board and authorised by those not covered. It has been reported that one company changed its Memorandum to allow the company to take out such a policy.

The exact cover of such a policy should be examined. It will usually exclude dishonesty, fraud, slander, libel, pollution and any actions resulting from a Director seeking to benefit personally. As indicated above, if a Director was found to be guilty of wrongful trading that would probably be classed as dishonesty and no claim could be made. On the other hand, if a Director was accused of Wrongful Trading but acquitted then the legal costs etc. associated with the case and borne by him would be claimable.

The Insolvency Act

In 1855 when limited liability protection was introduced it was ridiculed as a 'rogues' charter' and suggestions were made that the development was 'a means of devising the encouragement of speculation, overtrading and swindling', as many felt that the shareholders (i.e. the real risk takers) were being unfairly protected at the expense of the creditors whilst the 'protection' of the disclosure of information was thought to be of little value. This was to some extent true since in the event that the company failed, although the shareholders would lose their stake, their losses were likely to be smaller than the losses incurred by the creditors. Companies were required to file their accounts and also to indicate whether the assets referred to in such accounts were available generally to the creditors. A creditor could inspect the accounts and would be able to form an opinion regarding the value of the assets available to finance his debt. However, very often in order to finance its operations a company will borrow from (say) a bank, who will require it to provide security for the loan. The lender can create a charge over certain assets. Then, should the company fail, the assets over which a charge has been created cannot be used to satisfy debts other than those owed to the lender taking the charge. This has the effect of reducing the value of the assets available to the other creditors. Accordingly all such transactions must also be notified to the Registrar of Companies and placed on public display. Under the Companies Act 1989 changes were proposed to the method of registering such charges but to date these changes have not been implemented despite two rounds of consultations. However, such information is only of value if it is filed properly and within the required time which, in some cases, proved not to be the case. Thus, to some extent, the mid 19th century critics were correct – if only because the attitude to filing information was low key and there were until very recently very few sanctions for those companies and Directors who ignored the legal obligations – or filed so late that the information was useless for control purposes. In 1986 the Insolvency Act was passed in an effort to rectify the position by attaching considerable and personal penalties to those Directors who abused the limited liability status at the expense of their creditors. The Act created two offences – Wrongful Trading and Fraudulent Trading.

Wrongful trading occurs when Directors continue to allow the company to trade when there seems no possibility of it being able to settle its creditors' accounts within a reasonable time of them becoming due. In such circumstances the Directors are taking on credit with the perception of, or in the knowledge that, they may not be able to pay for it. This is tantamount to fraud. At the very least this means that they are misleading their creditors since the latter have no means of knowing the true financial position of the company (even if accounts have been filed they are probably so far out of date as to be meaningless). If the company then fails and the Receivers or Liquidators feel that the Directors had traded wrongfully then, as part of the report to the Department of Trade and Industry that they are obliged to make, they are required to state this. The DTI can then decide whether to take action against the Directors. If action is taken and the Court agrees, then those Directors held to be responsible may be required to contribute personally to the assets available to a Receiver or Liquidator to attempt to satisfy the creditors. In one case two Directors were required to contribute £75,000 each from their personal funds in such circumstances. The moment when a company started trading wrongfully may be easier to assess with hindsight than at the time it occurs, particularly as the Directors may at that time have their attention on attempts to save the company. It seems likely that it is possible to start to trade wrongfully almost by default although in such a case it may be that the Directors would not be found culpable.

If a company is getting into financial difficulties it is essential that the Directors take actions (such as those set out in the checklist below) since inaction (which could be regarded as negligence) could attract liability for wrongful trading.

Protecting one's position

1. Take advice – and act upon it – from auditors etc.

2. Cease trading and call a creditors meeting (whilst the immediate reaction may be horror at letting creditors know that they might not be paid, in fact the creditors are almost the last people who want the company to fail and usually are prepared to assist to try to rescue something from the situation). This emulates the old story 'if you owe the bank £5,000 and have no money – you have a problem; if you owe the bank £5,000,000 and have no money – the bank has a problem'.

3. Appoint an Administrative Receiver (in fact this option usually belongs to a bank which has taken a charge over the company's assets).

4. Petition the Court for the appointment of an Administrator (this is only likely to be an option if there are funds available that will enable the company to attempt to trade out of the situation.

5. Raise loans, source additional capital, merge with another organisation, amalgamate, seek a new owner (the purpose of all of these is to enable the company to have access to additional working capital).

6. Throughout all activity, make a note (and date) of everything done so that should action be taken, the Directors can show that they were being proactive in their efforts to save the company. Receivers and Liquidators are required to report to the DTI on every company failure and depending on their findings the DTI may take action against Directors. Having available a log of all activity (composed at the time – not later) could be a valuable piece of evidence of the efforts being made.

Fraudulent trading occurs when a company fails following deliberate action to defraud the creditors. In this case unlimited fines and imprisonment can be imposed on the Directors responsible.

Summary checklist

✓ Require preparation and regular updating of all legislation affecting the company and its operation.

✓ Determine the range of liabilities of Directors and develop principles to minimise such exposure.

✓ Require employees to abide by liability minimising rules.

✓ Ensure all officers understand their personal obligations under Insolvency Act.

✓ If in danger of trading wrongfully, keep detailed log of all actions taken to rectify the position.

chapter four

Scaling the peak

Appointment – and status

Eligibility for appointment

Whilst most Director appointees will be perfectly entitled to take up their post certain people cannot be Directors (see the checklist below) and, should such an appointment be attempted, can be disqualified from acting.

Persons unable to act as Directors

- Those who have passed the age limit i.e. 70. This ban applies to PLCs and their subsidiaries only and even then it is not an absolute bar to their appointment. If their shareholders approve it (and any re-appointment brought about by retirement by rotation) then the appointment will be valid. However, it has been stated by bodies representing institutional share investors that reasons should be given for the proposal.

- Those who are or become bankrupt. Again this does not constitute a complete bar as the approval of the Court can be sought to the appointment, which, if forthcoming, can validate it.

- Those who are or become insane.

- Any person who has been convicted of wrongful trading or who has been convicted under the Insolvency or Company Directors' Disqualification Acts.

- Any person who has been responsible for the persistent late filing of documents and the Court has made a disqualification order. (Where Directors are barred from acting by legislation the Court will normally specify a disqualification period.)

Some companies' Articles require Directors to acquire a number of the company's shares to 'qualify' them to act as a Director. If so the Director is not validly appointed until the shares are acquired and any acts taken as a Director prior to such acquisition may be invalid and the Director could require liability for them.

. . . .

A register of disqualified persons is maintained by, and can be inspected at, the offices of the Registrar of Companies. This register shows the names and dates of birth of disqualified Directors, the Court which made the order, and the date of the order's expiry.

Appointment of a Director

Those who are eligible for appointment are usually appointed by the Board (i.e. effectively co-opted by what may be regarded as a self-perpetuating body). However, all Director appointments are subject to shareholder approval so that a new Director only holds office until the next following general meeting at which the shareholders must be asked for their approval of the appointment. All Directors hold their authority and position by virtue of the power of the shareholders and the principles and procedure by which this power is exercised and the Directors can act is set out in the Articles which will also govern the size of the Board. Provided they do not infringe any restrictions in the Articles, the Directors can co-opt and appoint as many new Directors as they wish. Usually the re-election of a Director (either retiring because of recent appointment or by rotation) will be a formality but it is possible that the shareholders could vote against the re-election.

The actual appointment of a Director is effected in various stages as set out overleaf.

Appointment procedure

a) (Subject to any requirements in the Articles) the Board resolve to appoint X with effect from a stated date.

b) This decision should be recorded clearly and comprehensively in the Minutes.

c) The Director is invited to accept the appointment and, assuming he does, must provide personal details of himself.

d) These personal details (which comprise name (and any former names), private address, date of birth, occupation, details of other Directorships held in the past five years) and the date of appointment must be recorded in the company's Register of Directors and Secretaries and also on Form 288 which must be completed and sent to the Registrar of Companies.

e) In addition to the data set out in d) above, Form 288 contains a statement that the appointee consents to act as a Director which must be signed by the Director himself.

f) The form must be signed by a serving Director or the Company Secretary and filed with the Registrar within 14 days of the appointment. As with all filing it is prudent to obtain a receipt from the Registrar.

g) The Director must notify the company of any shares he owns in the company and of all changes to any shareholding. These details must be recorded by the company.

h) The Director must also notify (and constantly update) the company of any interest he may have in any business conducted by the company and this must be recorded (as must any later changes – see notification of interests opposite).

i) At the next following General Meeting the Director must retire and, assuming he so wishes, offer himself for re-election by the shareholders.

Notification of interests

All newly appointed Directors must declare any interests in parties with whom the company does business and/or through which they might benefit personally. Thus, if as well as being a Director of the subject company the new Director is also a Director or shareholder of (say) a supplier to the company he must declare that interest. The Director should then refer to the Articles to check the position regarding his interest. The requirements laid down by the Articles can vary from company to company. Thus there could be any of the following:

i)   A complete bar on the interest which must then be terminated (one would hope this would have been considered prior to the appointment to avoid embarrassment)

ii) A bar on the Director profiting from the interest (in that case he would need to pass any profits to the company)

iii) The interest may be allowed to continue but the Director would be prohibited from speaking and/or voting during any discussion of the matter at a Board Meeting

iv) The interest may be allowed to continue and, subject to reminding the members of the Board before making any comment, the Director may be allowed to speak and/or vote on it

v)   The interest may be allowed to continue without restrictions on speaking, voting etc., and/or allowing any profit to be retained.

1) It is most important that the requirements of the Articles are known and strictly adhered to. Failure to declare an interest renders the Director liable to substantial fines.

2) Whether a Director who has an interest is allowed to form part of the quorum for the effecting of that item of Board business needs to be checked. If the Articles state that the Director cannot be counted as part of the quorum and the quorum exceeds the number of other Directors present this may invalidate any decision.

Personal interest

The foregoing sets out the obligations that the Director has to the company. However, such an appointment is a two way process and the appointee needs to make certain checks on the company for which he is now taking personal (if shared) responsibility. The following checklist highlights various areas and aspects concerning which the new or prospective Director requires information.

Appointee's personal checklist

a) Obtain complete delineation of terms of appointment, service agreement, duties, reporting structure, etc. Check appointment has been made correctly and evidenced in the Minutes.

b) Check how payments of fees, expenses, salary etc., are to be made. (See below re question of relation-ship between a Director being an 'officer of the company' and an 'employee'.)

c) Obtain copy of latest accounts and management accounts (and any supplementary information) to enable appointee to consider financial state of company – if not previously supplied.

d) Obtain copy of Articles of Association to determine the powers (and restriction of powers) of Directors and officers, and copy of Minutes of Board for previous year and company for previous five years to check a) compliance and b) alterations to Articles.

(Note: This check will also provide valuable background information on the tactics and strategy adopted by the Board, and disclose any authorities granted by the Board on an individual or committee basis, which may require further information, etc.)

e) Check statutory file regarding submission of documentation to Registrar of Companies – inspect last Annual Return. Provide statutorily required information for filing record of own appointment if not already done.

f) Check statutory books for up to date entries.

g) Obtain copy of Directors' and Officers' Liability insurance policy and of renewal note. Check exact wording and cover.

h) Check situation regarding application and policing of internal procedures to minimise liability (see Chapters 3 and 8).

i) Obtain copy of all loan notes, guarantees, charges, etc.

j) Check any requirement for qualification shareholding, and, if there is – acquire such shares.

(Note: It may be that the appointment cannot become effective until such shares have been acquired.)

k) Prepare a list of companies and/or matters in which the appointee has an interest, and with which the company may be trading or negotiating. These potential conflicts of interest must be disclosed within five days of appointment (and subsequently when they arise). Whether they are allowed to subsist, and/or the

Director can vote on any such matter, and/or take any profit made from such interests must be checked with the Articles (see above).

l)   Check other Board member's interests are noted and what they are.

m) Establish whether any shadow Director(s) exist, and, if so, that their details are recorded in the various registers etc.

n)   Check whether any Directors are nominees of corporate shareholders and have any enhanced voting rights at Board Meetings.

o)   Request copy of any code of ethics or equivalent, confidentiality undertaking etc., applicable to Directors and/or senior members of the management of the company (see Chapter 9).

p)   Request schedule of Board Meetings and arrangements for obtaining information for discussion/decision at such meetings.

and so on.

Status – officer or employee?

As stated in Company Law a Director is an officer of the company. Once again although the term is used its meaning is unclear. The origins of Directorships lie in the days of 'joint ventures' before the creation of the limited liability company. In those days the role of the entrepreneur (the equivalent of the shareholder) and that of the Director tended to be blurred – often both functions were conducted by the same person. Obviously those that worked for the organisation were the equivalent of modern day employees (then regarded as 'servants') but entrepreneurs could not be similarly regarded. With the advent of limited liability Company Directors tended to be wealthy individuals who had no need of a salary but were content to take their reward as fees or by sharing in the profits, i.e. as dividends. Again they were not employees. Most modern day Directors are not in the same position as either their shareholders or their employees – although their positions may contain elements of both interests. They will normally regard their work as a Director in the same way, albeit at a more senior level, as that of a manager. The question of a Director being an employee as well as an 'officer' therefore needs to be addressed.

This problem has come before the courts on a number of occasions and a résumé of recent decisions is set out in checklist below.

Employment status of Directors

a) In *McLean v Secretary of State for Employment*, a Managing Director (and major shareholder) had no written contract with the company for which he had raised money by mortgaging his house. He was salaried – like his employees and paid PAYE and Class 1 NI contributions. The company became insolvent and Mr McLean applied to be paid redundancy pay as had his employees. The Employment Appeals Tribunal (EAT) held that he was not an employee and could not claim a redundancy payment.

b) In the cases of *Buchan v Secretary of State for Employment* and *Ivey v Secretary of State for Employment*, the EAT held that a controlling Director could not be an 'employee' for the purposes of employment legislation and thus in neither case could the Directors claim redundancy payments from the State when their companies became insolvent. Further, in the case of *Heffer v Secretary of State for Trade and Industry* the EAT held that an individual with a 70 per cent shareholding in a company was not an employee.

In making the decisions in the first two cases the EAT made the following findings:

- A limited company is a distinct legal entity from its shareholders and Directors

- A Director of a limited company may enter into and work under a contract of employment with that company

- A shareholder of a limited company may enter into and work under a contract of employment with that company.

However the EAT went on to point out that a controlling shareholder is able to prevent his or her own dismissal from the company and thus that person falls outside the class of persons who are intended to be protected by the arrangements for guaranteeing redundancy payments in the event of employer insolvency.

Note: These findings have to some extent been overturned by the decision in the case of _Fleming v Secretary of State for Trade & Industry_ where the Court of Session held that there is no rule of law that states that a majority shareholder cannot also be an 'employee'. This finding was confirmed by the EAT in the case of _Secretary of State for Trade & Industry v Bottrill_. The fact that someone has a majority shareholding is only one relevant factor in determining whether they also have employment status.

c) In the case of _BMK Holdings Ltd v Logue_, the EAT held that when Mr Logue was dismissed by the shareholders as both Chairman and chief executive, all his duties being bound up with his appointment as a Director, this effectively terminated his employment as well as the office. The EAT went on to comment that there was no absolute rule as to whether a Director was an employee – the facts of each case need to be examined.

The service contract

Accordingly there is nothing to stop a Director, even if he is also a shareholder (and possibly even a majority shareholder), being an employee in addition to being an officer and, assuming he works full-time for the company it would seem to be appropriate for the company to 'employ' him as both Director and employee. In that case it would seem logical for the appointment to be evidenced by a service contract which addresses both aspects of the relationship.

Service/employment contract

The usual service agreement/contract negotiated between the Director and the company specifies the salient details of the relationship. In many instances these items will be identical to that found in the average employment contract – pay, holiday, title and duties, sickness benefit, notice and termination and so on. The contract will often contain restrictions on the work that can be undertaken immediately after its termination which may make it somewhat more restrictive than those for an ordinary employee. Caution is needed in trying to incorporate restrictions on Directors (or other senior personnel) regarding leaving to work for competitors etc. Any clauses regarded as penalty clauses will probably prove to be enforceable. Thus, whilst a company may be able to require repayment of (for example) the cost of bought-in training since that could be argued to be an identifiable loss, they would not be able to insert a clause requiring the Director to repay (for example) three months pay should he not give the required notice, since it is unlikely (although not impossible) that they could prove that level of loss.

In addition, any clause which could be regarded as a restraint of trade clause may prove to be ineffective. As a rule of thumb a prohibition in time of around three/six months before working for a competitor is probably the maximum enforceable. During such a period of 'garden leave', the company would be responsible for paying the Director the salary agreed under the contract. Bans on soliciting custom, staff etc., are also best limited to three/six months.

Limitations

In the case of *Dentmaster (UK) Ltd v Kent*, the Court of Appeal held that a clause prohibiting (for six months after he left), an employee from soliciting any of those who had been customers during the six months prior to the termination of his employment and any of those customers with whom he had dealt during the whole of his employment was enforceable.

The twin relationship

Reflecting the twin relationship referred to above, ideally such a joint 'service/employment' contract should specify:

- That the subject is an employee as well as a Director, and

- That it is the 'principal statement' required under the Employment Rights Act 1996 as well as being a service contract.

It might also stipulate that termination of either relationship (i.e. Director or employee), from whatever cause, terminates the other relationship simultaneously and automatically, and that, in the event of damages being claimed under the service contract, part of such damages would be regarded as extinguishing part or all of any claims made under protection of employment legislation. Legal advice should be taken to ensure proper drafting of the appropriate clauses.

If this proposal is adopted it should simplify the situation should the person cease being a Director. For example, many Directors are required to retire by rotation, at the company's Annual General Meeting and to offer themselves for re-election. Should the shareholders either refuse to re-elect or simply dismiss the Director, this will almost certainly entail an action for breach of the service contract, but the situation regarding their employment rights may remain unclear. Indeed, if the person has duties other than their duties as a Director, it could be argued that these (and thus the person's employment by the company) continue, regardless of the cessation of the appointment as a Director, which would hardly be in anyone's interests. Conversely, although perhaps somewhat unlikely, a Director with other responsibilities could 'resign' from those employment obligations one day, and stroll back into the company to attend a Board Meeting the following day – which would be even less in the company's interests.

So difficult can these situations become, that a number of companies not only address the twin relationship in one contract but also insert a clause which, in the event of termination of the contract, grants to the company a power of attorney giving it the right to act as if it were the Director. Thus the company would then be able to sign a resignation letter and any other documents which, in the event of a dispute, the Director would no doubt refuse to sign in order to retain a bargaining power. Granting such power would not restrict the right of the Director to take action under the service contract. (At least one company requires its Directors to sign an undated letter of resignation on appointment – a move which hardly generates confidence at such a time!)

Specimen service/employment contract

In the checklist below is shown a draft service/employment contract for a Director. It must be stressed that the detailed requirements and terms to be included vary according to individual companies and specific legal advice should be taken.

Directors service/employment contract

This Agreement is made this day ...... of 199....../200......, between [the company] of [address] (the company) and .... (the executive).

It is hereby agreed that:

1. The company shall employ the executive as [title, list of duties, etc.] and the executive shall serve the company commencing the day ...... of 199 ....../ 200 ...... (the commencement date) for a rolling period of a maximum of three years so that (unless either party shall have given written notice of termination of this contract) the period shall be extended by a further one year on each anniversary of the commencement date.

   The appointment of the executive as Director and employment of the executive shall otherwise continue until the occurrence of:

   a) The last day of the month in which falls the executive's 65th birthday, or

   b) Three months from the date on which either party shall give to the other three months notice of termination in writing. For the purposes of employment legislation the date continuous employment commenced was [date], or

   c) The passing by the shareholders of a resolution removing the executive as a Director, which will simultaneously bring to an end the employment of the executive, or

   d) Summary dismissal as a result of gross misconduct committed either as a Director or as an employee which will simultaneously bring to an end the other relationship between the parties without compensation.

The executive hereby grants a power of attorney in favour of the company authorising it to sign the required forms evidencing such removal as resignation from the post of Director, and all ancillary matters, notwithstanding any rights the Director may have under this agreement.

2. The executive shall during the continuance of this agreement well and faithfully serve the company and use his/her utmost endeavours to promote the interests of the company and its' shareholders, giving it at all times the full benefit of his/her knowledge, skill and ingenuity, and shall perform all his/her duties as may from time to time be assigned or vested in him/her by the Board of Directors of the Company (the Board).

3. The executive shall during the continuance of this agreement devote the whole of his/her time and attention to the duties of the appointment (unless prevented from so doing by illness). He/she shall not, and shall cause his/her spouse and immediate family not to, directly or indirectly enter into, or be concerned in any manner (other than with the consent in writing of the Board or as a minority shareholder in a company quoted on a public stock exchange or bourse) with any company or organisation deemed to be (at the discretion of the Board) a competitor of the company.

4. The duties covered by this agreement shall be mainly carried out at the head office for the time being of the company, but the Director will be expected to travel to all company locations and elsewhere on company business and may be required to relocate within a [250 mile] radius of [London].

5. During the continuance of this agreement the company shall pay the executive (monthly) at the rate of £   per annum or such other rate as may

from time to time be agreed by the Board and will provide (at the cost of the company) a private motor car to the equivalent of   . [Exact terms of allocation and use of car are usually inserted here.]

6. In addition to remuneration, the executive will be entitled to reimbursement of all travelling, hotel and other expenses properly and reasonably incurred in the exercise of these duties and supported, as far as possible, by VAT receipts and invoices.

7. The executive will be entitled to [   ] days holiday in each year (exclusive of public or Bank Holidays) at such times as may be agreed by the Board.

8. In the event of the executive falling sick and being unable to perform the duties, the company will continue to pay the normal salary (for the time being) for a maximum of [   ] days in any one year. Should incapacity exceed such a period, further payment(s) will be at the discretion of the Board.

9. Should the executive become unable (by reason of incapacity, imprisonment etc.) to adequately perform the duties, or fail or neglect to perform the duties, or breach any of the provisions of this Agreement, then the company may forthwith determine this Agreement without notice as previously stipulated.

10. The executive shall not, without the consent in writing of the company, divulge to any other person, firm or company, and shall use his/her best endeavours to prevent the publication to any other person, firm or company of any information concerning the business or its' finances or any of the secrets, dealings, transactions or affairs of or relating to the company.

11. The executive acknowledges receipt of the company's Code of Ethics and undertakes to abide by the requirements thereof.

[12. The executive acknowledges receipt of the company's Stock Exchange listing agreement and undertakes to abide by the requirements thereof.]

13. The whole interest of the executive in any inventions emanating as a result of his/her employment by the company shall become the absolute property of the company without any payment being due to the executive.

14. Upon the termination of this Agreement (whether by effluxion of time or otherwise) the executive shall not (without the express written permission of the company) for a period of six months thereafter be connected with, or take part in the management of, or advise or direct, another business whose activities could conflict with the activities of the company. In addition the executive will not for a period of six months from such termination, solicit or take away any staff, custom, or business under the control of the company at the time of the termination.

15. Any notice or other document required to be given under this agreement shall be deemed to be served if it is sent by recorded delivery:

• by the company to the executive at his/her last recorded home address, or

• by the executive to the company via the Chairman or Company Secretary at their last recorded home address.

Signatures of parties

Witnesses

Notes:

1. It is usual for such a document to be treated as a deed and sealed on behalf of the company rather than simply signed. Companies are now allowed to dispense with the seal and instead to have such documents 'signed as a deed' (which wording should appear somewhere on the document) by two Directors or a Director and the Company Secretary, or in Scotland by a Director and a countersignatory. It may be preferable if the subject of the service agreement is not one of the company signatories.

2. Termination of such an agreement may give rise to compensation, which unlike that paid to other employees must be approved by shareholders and noted in the company's Report & Accounts.

3. Often service agreements will require the subject not to work for a competitor for a set period after termination of employment which may mean the company has to continue payment (and to provide all benefits due under the contract) and, unless the contract specifies, provide work during that period – the decisions in the cases of *William Hill Organisation Ltd v Tucker and Hutchings v Coinseed* for the term of this so-called 'garden leave' period.

4. All service contracts made with Directors are governed by law in that they must be made available for inspection by shareholders for two hours each working day.

Summary checklist

✓ Every appointment of a Director needs complete and comprehensive attention.

✓ All Directors must notify interests existing at time of appointment and thereafter notify all changes.

✓ New or prospective Directors should complete a checklist ensuring they have sufficient information regarding the appointment.

✓ Determine the employment status of Directors and reflect all items relating to both relationships in a single contract.

chapter five

'Ill met' – without method

Procedures for effective Board Meetings

Determining the aims of Board Meetings

Agendas

Aims

Procedure at meetings

Summary checklist

Determining the aims of Board Meetings

Open for business

Company law places no obligation on Directors to meet as a Board, or even for regular informal meetings of the Directors to be held. Perhaps more correctly it could be said that it carries no explicit requirements in this regard, although there are certainly implicit requirements that the Directors will meet and make decisions whether formally or informally, since should they fail to control the operation of the company they could be held to be in breach of their duty as Directors (see the *Dorchester Finance Co v Stebbing* case in Chapter 2).

Realistically most Directors will meet and discuss the conduct of the company with their colleagues and in most companies of any size or where there are more than (say) three Directors, this control is best exercised by holding regular meetings. Indeed, in most companies a considerable amount of the work of most Directors revolves around meetings – Board Meetings, meetings of committees appointed by the Board or meetings to discuss their own operational responsibilities. Irrespective of their level, all meetings should consider data, discuss proposals, contentions or conclusions arising from the data and make decisions. There is a saying that 'meetings take Minutes and waste hours' – if so it is because three key aspects of successful (i.e. effective) meeting administration may not be playing their required part:

- The aims of the meeting have not been clearly set

- The Chairman has not kept the attention of the meeting to the aims determined, and

- The Secretary has not ensured the meeting flows smoothly with everyone advised of all details regarding business previously noted for discussion (for example, by the provision of a dynamic agenda – see over).

In addition, the ethos of the organisation needs to be tuned to the accomplishment of business via meetings. This may be easier said than done since in some organisations meetings seem to be held for 'meetings sake' and in fact far from stimulating and generating swift decisions, they may be used as a means for delaying decisions and ensuring when taken that no one individual can be held responsible for their effect. This may be acceptable for some 'junior' meetings but it is unlikely for it to be acceptable for Board Meetings.

Agendas

Every meeting should have an aim – if only 'to review progress since the last meeting and consider how this impacts the attainment of short and long-term aims'. To ensure the meeting adheres to its aim it may be advisable to state it at the commencement of the agenda and to compose the agenda in such a way that it delineates the business requiring decisions which meet the aim. Too often the composition of an agenda is given insufficient attention and serves as little more than a notification to those required to attend of the date and time of the meeting rather than creating an awareness of subject matter that needs research, deliberation and decision.

Inevitably the construction of an agenda will depend very much on the type of meeting required – but equally the efficiency of the meeting can depend how constructively the agenda is compiled. If it is a regular monitoring meeting it could comprise items drawn from the sources set out in the checklist below:

Sources for agenda items

a) An annual list of items to be considered at set times (e.g. the dividend, preliminary announcement)

b) Items to be considered or reconsidered requested from the previous or earlier meetings

c) New business arising since the previous meeting out of the operation of the organisation

d) Items requested to be considered by members (individual house rules may apply to these items – e.g. they may be required to be approved by the Chairman prior to inclusion)

e) Regular reports (accounts, cash forecast, contracts, etc.)

f) Market, economic or legal changes affecting the business

g) Statutorily (or similarly) required items (e.g. approval of the report of the Directors and annual accounts for submission to the AGM, dividend recommendation, etc.)

h) Original material, possibly generated by the Chairman as a result of his responsibility for driving the meeting and the company forward.

Alternatively a meeting may be required to consider a particular subject. In this case there is greater scope for determining the extent of the deliberations, the aim and even the duration of the meeting by generating what can be termed a 'dynamic agenda'.

Dynamic agenda

AGENDA

for an [informal executive] meeting to be held on:

[date one week ahead]

in the Company Boardroom at 2.00 p.m. prompt

Subject: Employee absenteeism

Aim of meeting:

To devise and implement [up to five] tactics or initiatives for immediate implementation which will have the effect of reducing absenteeism to near or below the industry average.

Items for discussion:

1. To consider monthly reports of staff absenteeism over past 12 months (see analysis attached).

2. To compare such reports with analyses of absenteeism throughout the industry (see report from [Industry] Trade Association attached).

3. To consider whether there are special reasons for this company's poor performance, and if so what can be changed/improved to ensure a reduction.

4. To determine [five or more] methods to ensure such a reduction. Members will be expected to attend with ideas for consideration at the meeting, such ideas must be capable of implementation within 14 days.

Administration:

The meeting duration will be two hours. No interruptions or messages.

Attendance:

Group Finance Director (Chairman), Personnel Director, Company Nurse, Company Secretary, Works Manager.

Notes:

a) Setting the meeting a week ahead should allow ample thinking time

b) Providing internal statistics with external comparisons sets the problem in context with the delay before the meeting allowing time for assimilation of the data

c) Requesting members ideas should assist accountability

d) Stating that there must be no interruptions not only allows meeting members to brief their staff accordingly but also underlines the importance attached to the subject by the Chairman. It is not unknown for some meeting attenders to arrange for deliberate interruptions to meetings either to enable them to escape some agenda items or simply to try to bolster their own importance

e) The tone and structure of the agenda itself seeks to demonstrate that action is required. It implies an urgency reflecting that of the subject.

With regular meetings (e.g. Board Meetings), an agenda should always follow a set format and order, whilst the grouping of like items under general headings may assist the logical 'flow' of the business of the meeting. Setting out under each item the aim of the business (for example a draft resolution) should help concentrate the mind on what needs to be addressed.

Timetable

Certain business needs to be transacted at set times of the year and the timing of these requirements should be reflected in the list of meeting dates which should be prepared for at least a year ahead. This could include firm dates for (say) nine months, with suggested dates for later meetings which would be confirmed by an updated timetable issued on (say) a rolling six month basis. This list should incorporate reference to such business, e.g. dividend payment, preliminary announcement and report publication dates etc. Ideally meeting dates should not be altered to avoid:

a) Members finding that although they could have attended on the original date they cannot make the amended date, and

b) Those required to originate and submit items and reports for the Board to alter what can be complex reporting procedures.

Ideally, Board Meetings should not be cancelled although a short postponement may be inevitable on occasion. In most companies there is routine business which needs to be authorised or considered and cancellation may mean that required authority is not obtained, either leading to delay or possibly commitment without proper authorisation.

Timing and despatch of agenda

There is no current legal requirement to generate an agenda for Board Meetings or any prescription regarding its contents. Commercial pressures (apart from the need already highlighted to be able to demonstrate to shareholders and others that proper control of the company is being undertaken) however will usually dictate that all Board Meetings should be properly convened. The simplest way of effecting this is by sending a properly composed and issued agenda with back up data to every member in good time, so that Directors are:

a) Able to exercise the required control

b) Able to make informed judgements on the matters requiring decisions, and

c) Have information of the current company strategy and tactics (drawn from interfacing with their colleagues) to apply to their own direct responsibilities.

It is perhaps worth emphasising that ALL Directors should be sent an agenda and supporting documentation. This should apply even when a Director has indicated that he will be unable to attend and/or will be out of the country (when Company Law states that there is no obligation to send him an agenda). In this way the Director will receive not only the agenda but also the supporting documentation. Since most Boards operate under a kind of 'continuum', with policy developing in reaction to events, by reading the documentation and the Minutes, even Directors who were unable to be present at a meeting should remain comprehensively briefed and updated.

Ideally an agenda should be despatched at least seven working days prior to the meeting and be accompanied by all relevant documents. Unless this occurs many members will attend not having read the papers, leading in turn either:

- To decisions being taken based on incomplete knowledge, or

- Using valuable meeting time whilst individuals check points in documents only received just before or even at the meeting. Where papers do need to be given to members late a résumé of the salient points should be requested as a covering sheet.

There are instances where data relating to contentious matters are deliberately held back and tabled at the meeting so that the sponsor can try to gain acceptance without proper consideration or discussion. This kind of approach should be stopped by the Chairman since it is a denial of the right of Directors to be informed on matters on which they must make decisions. It also acts against the principle of the Board working collectively as a team.

Aims

Meetings exist to take decisions. The Chairman/meeting should establish what decisions are required and by when. These should be stated when the body is set up (e.g. as its terms of reference) and possibly repeated at the commencement of the meeting to encourage focussing of attention. Where use is made of a dynamic agenda this principle can be reflected within the agenda itself.

Much of the Board's work will be a consideration of routine business – nevertheless this is still an aim forming part of the overall duty to drive the business forward (i.e. taking relatively low key decisions to improve performance etc.).

Composition and cost

Only those required to attend should be present since a meeting's length tends to be proportionate to the number present. Obviously all Directors, unless unavoidably absent, should attend but often a Board's numbers may be swelled by requesting the attendance of advisors – both internal and external (e.g. auditors etc.). Whilst the attendance of such persons may be essential for the proper consideration of individual items, they should be encouraged to attend only for the discussion of that item. If the Board is attended by persons whose contribution is unnecessary or irrelevant, the effectiveness of those required to be present and of the meeting as a whole can be diluted. Unfortunately attendance at a meeting can sometimes be regarded as an indication of importance which can then become an enticement to attend even when there is no point or requirement.

Calculating the cost per minute of those present at the meeting (based on annual salary plus oncosts) may encourage a crude cost-benefit analysis of the value of the decisions reached. Consideration of such cost may concentrate the mind on the meeting's composition. All members should be encouraged to make effective contributions that are concise yet comprehensive. The meeting exists to take decisions, and whilst some dialogue is necessary to explore all the ramifications of each item of business, allowing such dissection of data to become general discussions may be counter-productive. Against this,'brainstorming' should not be undervalued. However, if this is required (e.g. to determine new products, direction, strategy etc., or simply to help formulate the latest business plan) it should be on a properly structured basis – at a meeting (perhaps off premises) deliberately convened for the purpose.

Data

Reports, analyses and all other data required for consideration by the meeting should accompany the agenda (and be presented in the order of the agenda) or a note regarding late submission be appended thereto (see the checklist on page 100). Tabling a bulky or complex report should be avoided as decision-taking on its contents is likely to be uninformed. Where such data comprises bulky or complex reports, an accompanying précis of findings and/or recommendations may be useful. A rule that all reports should contain brief and prioritised recommendations and incorporate a requirement to analysis the effect of NOT proceeding in the way suggested, may encourage effective analysis and action. Whilst the aim of this is to ensure that the meeting has available the information required in order to make most appropriate decisions, the requirement to prepare a synopsis and recommendations and to consider a 'no progress' alternative can focus the mind and may even suggest further alternatives – that is achieve a dynamism of its own.

Procedure at meetings

Although the level of formality of the meeting will differ widely according to individual company preferences and custom, it is usual for all members to sign a book of attendance, and to address and speak through the Chairman, and for the Chairman to summarise the considered suggestions(s), before taking the 'sense' or decision of the meeting – usually by consensus, but occasionally by vote. Summarising the decision aids the accurate recording of the decision in the Minutes. In a Board Meeting each person (since they are obliged to be present) has a right to be heard on each subject, not least since the authority for the decisions depends on the collective responsibility of the Board as an entity.

Apologies for absence

Directors are under pressure (if only to be able to demonstrate that they are exercising the required control over the company and thus fulfilling their duty) to attend Board Meetings unless their absence is unavoidable (in Table A, a Director who absents himself without good cause from Board Meetings for six months or more can be removed from office by his colleagues). Failure to attend could lead to accusations of dereliction of the duties Directors were appointed to undertake (apart from rendering them liable for personal penalties should the company find itself in difficulties).

Thus it is important to record both who is present and who is absent. Many companies require their Directors to sign an attendance book for each meeting. In addition should they need to leave the meeting prior to its conclusion this fact should be noted in the Minutes – as should late arrival.

Quorum

If a quorum is required under the Articles, the Secretary should ensure these requirements can be met. If regular difficulty is experienced obtaining a quorum (for example the number of Directors is four and there is no wish to increase the size of the Board since it operates well, but the quorum is also four), the requirement in the Articles should be considered for review. One alternative to this would be to allow a non-quorate meeting to take place with all decisions arrived at being made 'subject to full Board ratification'. At the next following meeting at which a quorum is present all the acts and decisions arrived at by the non-quorate body can then be ratified. The problem with such a device is that if there is any appreciable time delay between meetings of the non-quorate body and the Board with a proper quorum any decisions may be held to be *ultra vires*. Legal advice should be taken. Whether Directors with interests in the subject matter can be counted as part of the quorum should also be checked to avoid the situation where decisions are made by a non-quorate Board with potential implications for those responsible.

Where the number of Directors is relatively low and the quorum required relatively high, care should be taken that a meeting which starts quorate does not become 'non-quorate' because a Director has to leave before its conclusion.

Where a Board is larger and requires specific matters to be considered by sub-committees, each of them should be given terms of reference including a quorum requirement.

Voting

Experience indicates that most business at Board Meetings is agreed by consensus. Given that, to be effective, the Board must act as a team and despite sometimes divergent views share a common aim, this may not be surprising. However, there may be occasions when consensus is not possible and a formal vote needs to be taken. The voting power of individual members needs to be checked against the terms of reference/appointment, for example:

a) The Chairman may be granted a second or casting vote in the event of an equality of votes

b) In some instances the Chairman only has a vote where there is an equality of votes

c) A Director with an interest in the subject under discussion may not have a vote (and may or may not be able to join in the discussion)

d) Where a Director(s) is/are 'nominee(s)', for example of a major corporate shareholder (or of the 'senior' partner in a joint venture company), they may have enhanced voting rights in particular circumstances, and so on. Once again the Articles need to be referred to, to ensure votes are properly exercised.

The effective meeting

Although the responsibility for the convening and running of Board Meetings lies predominately with, and should be delegated to the Company Secretary and reference should be made to Chapter 7 to review the Secretary's responsibilities in this area, ultimately Directors are responsible for all activities of the company. No activity is more important than that of running Shareholder and Board Meetings and every Director should be aware of the need to ensure that their meetings are effective, efficient and that all required business is reviewed and necessary decisions made.

Board Meetings should exist for one purpose only – to consider reports, data and business, thus enabling the Board to take decisions that will have the effect of driving the company forward to attain its aims. It should be obvious that to achieve this, those present need to be comprehensively briefed on the subject matters. This can be best achieved by ensuring that all reports, data and proposals are set before the members well in advance of the meeting so that they have time:

• To consider the content

- To think about it, and

- To make their own investigation or research on the subject, etc.

Inevitably there will be occasions when a report etc. has to be tabled – in such a case, members should be required to present the report amplified by a brief précis of findings and/or recommendations. The concept of providing a précis can be a valuable time-saver for other business – bearing in mind the responsibility on Directors to be aware of items that they might be asked to sign. (See the *D'Jan* case in Chapter 1). For this reason a 'Data submission checklist' may be helpful.

Data submission requirements

Timetable

1. A timetable for all required to attend and/or submit data to the meeting will be prepared on a rolling six month basis and issued by the Company Secretary.

2. Other than in the most exceptional instances, the timing of meetings will not be changed and any member unable to attend must let the Company Secretary know as soon as possible.

3. A member wishing to raise business at a Board Meeting must clear its inclusion with the Chairman ten working days before the meeting and, providing the Chairman has approved its inclusion, advise the Company Secretary of the need to add it to the agenda for the next meeting.

4. An agenda with supporting data should always be issued at least seven working days prior to a meeting.

Data required

1. All information and reports should be made available to the Company Secretary at least nine working days before the meeting.

2. All data should be submitted with the required number of copies. This number should be the number of persons entitled to receive the agenda plus any required to be sent out for information, plus, say, two spares.

- Some companies distribute Board reports (even confidential material) to senior executives. An approved distribution list needs to be compiled.

- Where it is usual for a number of documents to accompany the agenda, colour coding such documentation could be considered to aid swift reference during the meeting, although if the members keep their papers in 'agenda order' this should not be a problem.

3. If data is not available to meet the submission deadline a written note of its availability date must be given, the Chairman must be informed and notes of the expected date of receipt/issue and source entered on the agenda.

4. Those submitting data late must ensure it is conveyed directly to the meeting members prior to the meeting with the required number of spares given to the Company Secretary. Asking for data to be allowed to be tabled at the meeting, particularly if it consists of detailed, involved or lengthy reports may result in the item being 'left on the table' for consideration at a later meeting.

5. Documentation will always be presented in agenda order.

Presentation

1. Every item prepared for the [Board/committee] will be required to contain a standard covering sheet (see below).

2. Subsequent sheets may be presented in the format most suitable for the subject matter.

3. The utmost brevity, commensurate with the subject matter, should be employed. Commentary (other than the minimum necessary to explain approach etc.) should be avoided and facts and suppositions, and opposing data, suitably differentiated, must be presented clearly.

4. Source(s) of data should be referenced, and a summary used, rather than including such data as part of the submission.

5. The conclusions and recommendations that are required to be set out on the first page, must be clearly evidenced within the report.

6. Plain English should be used with jargon avoided. Where jargon is essential, a glossary accurately defining the terms used should be included.

7. A résumé of the effect of NOT proceeding with the proposals should be provided.

Supporting commentary

1. At the meeting, the report's originator or person responsible for the subject matter should be prepared to present the report, to answer questions from other members and generally to assist the meeting to come to a suitable decision regarding its content.

2. Should the meeting require amplifying documentation this must be provided in the same format as that used in the original report and submitted for the next following meeting (or as agreed at the meeting).

3. Proposers may be restricted to only one opportunity to support or promote the subject matter and should therefore cover all salient facts in their initial presentation.

   Note: This will entail marshalling all facts, data, comments and so on, balancing brevity against comprehensiveness, highlighting only the most important aspects and avoiding repetition, other than when necessary as a result of other members' questions.

4. Other meeting members should similarly endeavour to speak only once, putting forward their objections or comments in the same manner as set out in 3 above.

5. After such proposal and counter-comments, if the subject is of such import the Chairman may wish to encourage a short general discussion on the subject, otherwise the next move will be to summarise the content and take the sense of the meeting.

Decisions

1. Decisions will be summarised in the Minutes of the meeting. A synopsis for non-Board members will be communicated by the Company Secretary and/or the sponsoring member.

2. If referred back for reconsideration the decision will be supported by a copy and/or extract of the Minutes dealing with the subject which will include any conditions, timing, capital expenditure, and so on.

Draft covering sheet for data submitted:

Report title..................... Date of report.....................

Author/sponsoring dept..

Data to be considered by meeting...............................

Subject matter (aims of report/submission/etc.)

....

Recommendations
1...

2...etc.

Résumé of facts/contentions supporting recommendations
....

Résumé of facts/contentions contesting recommendations
....

Implications for organisation if not proceeded with
....

Capital expenditure implications......................................

....

Skill/personnel implications...

Timing required ....

....

Summary checklist

✓ Set up aims, purpose and ongoing future timetable for Board Meetings.

✓ Give the preparation of an agenda constructive attention to help the meeting reach suitable decisions.

✓ Convene meetings with sufficient notice for consideration of the data for the business to be conducted.

✓ Provide guidelines for the submission of data to be considered.

✓ Delineate procedures re attendance and absence, quorum, voting etc.

chapter six

Board without boredom

Preparation for and administration of Board Meetings

General preparation

Experience indicates that some Directors attend meetings and, whilst they may have read the papers provided, have made little preparation for the decision-making task concerning the subject matter. Scant attention to such preparation is dangerous since not only is there incomplete understanding, but also this may be based on inaccurate data. Investigating the data enhances understanding as well as enabling checks on its credibility and accuracy to be made. A Board which has worked together for some time may be able to 'take data as read' since they will understand the way each member thinks and know they can rely on the data being provided. However, even where such confidence exists it may be preferable for Board members to make their own investigations and even compile their own records simply since the process of making up one's own record tends to fix the facts in one's mind. In addition it is not unknown for some reports or proposals to provide a 'gloss' (i.e. a good case) for a particular project which suppresses information which could contradict data put forward to support the contentions. Ideally members of a close working unit such as a Board should avoid such tactics but realistically one needs to be aware that such tactics can be adopted.

One reason for recommending that all data is sent to Board members at least seven working days before the meeting is to enable members to study the proposals, to have the opportunity of asking the author for more information and to conduct their own independent investigations. The antithesis of this is the device already referred to where a bulky report is tabled and the Board is put under pressure to accept the recommendations without sufficient time to consider them or to make independent investigations. Whilst on occasions there may be no alternative the Chairman should insist that this is the exception to the rule – after all, ultimately the Directors could be personally responsible for their decisions and thus they need time to consider not just the recommendations put forward but also the 'knock-on' effects of such decisions.

Preparing effective reports

The decision making process will be assisted immeasurably if the reports being presented to the Board are:

- Effective – short and explicit

- Presented in a common format.

Report writing is an art which is often overlooked. The main problem is that those required to prepare a report often compose it from a particular angle – their own as the author – rather than from the ideal angle – that is the requirements of the reader. Yet a moment's consideration will reveal that if the reader doesn't understand the report there is only one person who is responsible – the writer who needs to compose it in a way that is conducive to the reader's comprehension, ideally at a first reading (bearing in mind that the time available to most Board members is limited). Reports should therefore be short, sharp and provoke attention, and following the layout suggested in the checklist below may be apposite.

Report composition guidelines

1. Providing a title for the report can allow the reader to gain instant guidance to content.

2. The author and date of the report should also be given to facilitate reference back.

3. The terms of reference or aim of the report should appear at the beginning of the report and it may assist if immediately under the aims or purpose the recommendations are also set out. This enables the reader to gain an immediate view of the opinion being adopted by the writer and places the content in perspective.

4. The main content of the report could comprise:

   - Background (i.e. the reason the report has been prepared)

- History (i.e. the developments that have led to a situation where a report is necessary)

- Methodology

- Data and research on which the contentions or recommendations are drawn

- Perspective data (i.e. it may assist consideration of a report on, say, a declining return on the company's capital investment, if the industry figures which either match or conflict with the company's own results are included).

5. The report should conclude with a repeat of the recommendations and may also incorporate a timetable or list of steps to be taken. If the writer of the report is not to be present when the report is read or considered it may help the readers to explain the recommendations thus pre-empting some questions.

6. Whilst the content of a report is the most important consideration, its presentation is also important. A sound report can be damaged by poor presentation whereas a merely adequate report can be made to look far more impressive if it is well-presented:

- Graphics (where these arise naturally from the text and can provide the reader with an instant view of the point being made) should be used – but not to excess.

- Jargon, unless the writer is certain that every reader will know the meaning, should be avoided. (If the writer is unsure of this but wishes to use jargon it may be safest to include a glossary of terms used.) Ordinary everyday English is the best language to use although often one reads reports that seem to have adopted a 'reportese' language which does little to aid comprehension! (Inveterate jargon users might be usefully advised of the correct meaning of jargon: the murmuring babble made by an infant (literal meaning 'without words') before it learns how to speak properly!)

- The likelihood of instant comprehension or of problems can be checked by submitting the report to a Fog Index – i.e. a check of the readability of the prose based on the length of sentences and complexity of the words used.

7. Where data has been drawn from sources which are themselves bulky it may be better simply to cross-reference to the source and to state where this can be found.

8. If the report consists of more than, say, six pages, it may help to include a list of contents. The effectiveness of a contents list (and of the report itself) can be aided by using key words or headlines throughout. Not only will this guide the reader to those parts of the report of most interest to them, it will also maintain interest which will also be stimulated by cutting up slabs of text into 'digestible chunks'.

Planning

Most of the Board's responsibilities entail a requirement to look to the future even though much of the data on which such decisions are required to be taken may be historical. Planning involves the Board in making reasoned guesses based on the information they have available to them as to likely events and situations and the company's possible reactions to those events. There are three essential needs in planning for future actions which are often overlooked:

a) The need to retain flexibility so that if what was anticipated does not develop in the way required an alternative approach is available

b) The need to take action quickly once it is obvious that things are not going the way they were planned and

c) The need to plan for things going wrong in the same way as planning in the expectation of things going well. Crisis or disaster planning (e.g. in the case of a fire, loss of key person, adverse media attention, etc.) is increasingly being adopted by Boards so that there is at least a checklist of possible actions or activities which can be considered immediately rather than time, likely to be at a premium when disaster strikes, being spent on such thoughts or over hasty actions being taken.

The shareholders of companies appoint Directors to drive their companies forward. Inevitably most decisions taken are more akin to a 'touch on the tiller' which steers the company in the best direction. However, at times major changes of direction may need to be taken to preserve the business of the company and/or to allow it to maximise its investment. Shareholders expect their Directors to take decisions and to plan for eventualities and it is at least arguable that the Board that does not make plans no matter how outline these may be, is failing in its duty to its shareholders. As already noted – a Board which is currently failing to investigate the effect of the 'millennium bug' on its computer systems, could be considered by its shareholders to be avoiding its obligations to plan and to drive the company forward.

Negotiation and powerplay

Board alliances – and disputes

The most effective and successful companies are probably those where the Board, whilst they may have individual differences, act as a cohesive team with shared aspirations and plans. Inevitably from time to time differences may arise and the Director who wishes to gain approval for a pet project will be somewhat short-sighted if he does not attempt to gain support from colleagues in advance of consideration of the matter at a Board Meeting. Seeking support, even if it entails a 'quid pro quo' from the other party may be a sensible way of approaching the matter. Few people like losing out or ending up on the wrong side, particularly in a public forum, and such public defeat may be avoided by broaching the subject with colleagues in advance, gaining their reactions and either toning down or altering aspects of the suggestion or, if there seems to be little support or total animosity, dropping the idea altogether.

Such a strategy has a number of advantages:

- It grants the member the reputation of being a good team player. Reputation and respect can help win arguments in meetings and dealing with a possibly controversial matter outside the meeting, particularly if it concerns or is raised with the Chairman, may well earn the instigator some prestige for future use, even though the actual subject matter gains no support on the present occasion.

- It avoids embarrassing the person as it could were it to be raised in open meeting. The position of that person, particularly if he is the Chairman, is thus protected. He can explain opposition or reaction in private, and possibly even in confidence, to the instigator, without the pressure of the meeting.

- It enables the instigator to gain some measure of the depth of feeling likely to be encountered were the matter to be raised in meeting. If the reaction is very hostile he can back off immediately.

• The concept itself is brought into the open. Whilst it may not gain support this time around, repeated references to the idea may ultimately win over those formerly antagonistic to it, particularly if later events are used to illustrate its' advisability.

Occasionally, however, despite all endeavours, antipathy can surface at a Board Meeting even leading to a situation where one Board member find themselves completely at odds with their colleagues. They may feel so strongly that they wish their dissent to be noted in the Minutes. Most Chairmen will try to avoid this, not least since it is breaking the cohesion of the Board team, but if the Director is adamant then a suitable minute should be included.

Appointing subcommittees

With a company of any size, requiring the Board to consider all the business can make the main Board Meeting over-lengthy and inefficient. This can be avoided by appointing committees of the Board (usually with power to co-opt other members) to consider certain aspects of the operations with reports of decisions only submitted to the Board for ratification.

Where such committees are appointed, their exact terms of reference, composition and quorum should be set out clearly. They should also be required to take accurate Minutes and to submit those Minutes to the Board so that any recommendations can be ratified or approved. Minute writing is an acquired art and if there is no person available to write up their Minutes this may be best done by the Company Secretary at the direction of the Chairman of the sub-committee. The Secretary should not object to writing such Minutes (even if he was not present at the meeting) provided it is made clear who was there and that they subsequently approve the Minutes as a true record.

Minutes – example and usage

Minute-taking is an art and, without practice few can compose reliable and accurate Minutes, which normally comprise only a résumé of the decisions taken. This however is for the meeting to decide and it may be preferable for the Minutes to provide details of the main arguments as well as the decisions. This can be dangerous since it can lead to dissent regarding the arguments put forward and generally the shorter and more succinct the Minutes the better. Most minute takers tend to write notes at the time and then write the full Minutes up from those notes.

To effect this if a further copy of the agenda is word processed but with spaces left after each item so that such notes can be inserted, the composition of the Minutes may be rendered more easily achieved.

Secretaries with experience of the way their Board thinks and acts may be able to develop what can amount almost to a 'pro forma' copy of the agenda which includes likely resolutions and decisions. This all aids the Secretary in restricting the amount of writing and allowing more concentration on the business being transacted. Although this process can lead to accusations that the Secretary is writing the Minutes before the meeting takes place, the advantage of having agenda and outline Minutes on one document sheet should not be underestimated. After all, if care has been taken in the composition of the agenda there should be a reasonably clear idea of the likely decisions that will be made and thus the composition of the Minutes. The aim of such a gambit, is not so much to manipulate the meeting as to make sure it achieves effectiveness, after all a draft is simply that.

Minutes must be a true, fair and accurate record. This is particularly important if the organisation needs to produce a certified copy of a minute to a third party, e.g. to evidence a signatory's authority to sign a contract.

Board Meeting Minutes

It is perhaps easier to consider the means of composing and advantages of having available well-written Minutes by reviewing a set of Minutes and highlighting particular aspects as is shown in the checklist below.

ANY COMPANY LIMITED   182(1)

MINUTES of a
BOARD MEETING held on 30th November 1998
at [address] at 10.00 a.m.

Present: XYZ (in the chair)
ABC
DEF
GHI

In attendance: JKL (Company Secretary)

(Mr. TSS, Auditor was in attendance for items covered by Minute 2i and ii)   (2)

An apology for absence due to illness was received from UVW. Those present signed the attendance book.   (3)

1.   Minutes

The Minutes of the Board Meeting held on 27th October 1998 previously distributed were taken as read, approved and signed.   (4)

2.   Shareholder matters

It was resolved that a share transfer covering 500 ordinary shares in the company from Mrs MNO to Mr PQR be and it hereby is approved and that a share certificate in the name of Mr PQR be issued and the required entries be made in the Register of Members. The Secretary was asked to write personally to Mr PQR welcoming him as a shareholder.

Action: JKL (5)

A report from the Company Secretary recommending that responsibility for the share registration work of the company be placed with Professional Share Registrars Ltd, from a date within the following three months was accepted and the terms of the contract approved. The Company Secretary was requested to make the necessary arrangements in liaison with the Chairman.   Action: JKL

(Mr DEF, having previously notified the company that he had a consultancy agreement with Share Registrars Ltd did not take any part in this discussion or vote on the proposal.)
(6)

3.   Finance

i)   Management accounts. The full set of management accounts for the month of October and the cumulative six months were tabled and discussed in detail. The favourable comparison with budget was welcomed, as was the Managing Director's report of a favourable Autumn trading period for which full comparative figures would be available shortly and his opinion that the trading and financial situation would continue to show improvement, both in real terms and against budget.

It was noted that the situation regarding discounts and promotional payments was still being clarified and additional controls would be introduced from the start of the new financial year.

A number of estimated provisions were listed for possible incorporation in the year end accounts.
Action: ABC

ii) Depreciation. It was agreed to change the company's accounting policies so that depreciation would be charged on vehicles, office equipment and computers @ 33.3 per cent p.a. straightline. It was noted that this change would have to be recorded in the Accounting Policies note to the next set of audited accounts.

iii) Capital expenditure.

   a) It was agreed that a further five product units at a cost of around £4000 each could be purchased on stages over the remainder of 1998 and the first six months of 1999 to allow the sale of [detail]. Mr UVW, whom failing the Company Secretary, would authorise each item bearing in mind the effect on cash flow. (7)

   b) The Chairman referred to Capital Expenditure Project form number 13/98 for the investment in [detail] which projected a first year return of 14 per cent rising to 17 per cent in year two on a fully absorbed basis. The project was approved for implementation no earlier than 31st January 1999.

Action: ABC

iv) Cash flow. The latest projection for the period ending 30th June 1999 was tabled, discussed and approved.

v) Investigations for the replacement of the company vehicles allocated to six area managers would be carried out. The guidance of the auditors as to the Company's and individual's tax situation would be sought.

Action: GHI

vi) Bank mandate. The Secretary reported that the company's bankers had requested that a new mandate on the main drawing account be completed.

It was resolved that the company operate the No 1 Main Drawing account in its name with the Finance Bank Plc on the terms and subject to the restrictions set out in a new mandate a copy of which initialled by the Chairman for the purposes of identification is attached to these Minutes, and that the Secretary be and he hereby is empowered to take such actions as might be necessary to give effect to this resolution.

Action: JKL (8)

vii) Borrowings. The Secretary reported that in the absence of Mr UVW he had negotiated an additional £100,000 overdraft facility with the Finance Bank on the same terms as the existing facility. This additional borrowing was available for the eight weeks from 1st April until end May 1999. Although he had expected to receive documentation requiring Board approval to evidence this borrowing this had not arrived before the meeting.

It was resolved that the Chairman, ABC and UVW (whom failing that, the Company Secretary) be and they hereby are empowered to sign such documents and take such actions to provide the company's bankers with the documentation they required in order to facilitate the advance of this additional borrowing requirement.

The Secretary was instructed to let each Board member have copies of the relevant items and documentation when these were to hand.

The Secretary confirmed that even with this additional borrowing the limits in the Articles had not been breached.

(9)

Action: XYZ, ABC, JKL

4.   Current trading

The Managing Director reported that [résumé of report ....]. An analysis showing the deterioration over a five year period of sales of the main product was tabled and it was agreed that the deadline for delivery of supplies of Project X needed to be brought forward to compensate for the expected shortfall in sales in the latter part of the calendar year.   Action: ABC

Mr DEF requested that his dissent from this course of action be noted in the Minutes with the note that in his opinion not enough was being done to incentivise the sales force and he had serious doubts concerning the effectiveness of the recently appointed sales manager.   (10)

5. Personnel

i) A report from the Divisional Director (Personnel) had been sent to all members and the contents were accepted. It was agreed that negotiations should commence with employee representatives to try to agree the wage increase with effect from 1st April 1999 along the lines outlined in the report.

ii) The Secretary reported that he had investigated the requirements of the current Health and Safety legislation regarding Fire Precautions in the Workplace and tabled a brief résumé of the additional action he felt it was necessary for the company to take in order to comply with the requirements. The Board requested him to obtain detailed cost estimates for the various requirements with, in each case, an indication of the proposed timetable for implementation of the recommendations.

Action: JKL

(At this point Mr DEF apologised and, with the Chairman's permission, left the meeting.)　　　　　　　　　(11)

6. Property

The following items were noted:　　　　　　　　　(12)

a) Little progress had been made on any of the pending rent reviews which would update the list accompanying the agenda for the meeting other than the following:

[Facility]: Approval was granted to a letter of response to the Landlords requesting that an extension to the user be agreed.

[Facility]: Evidence thought to be misleading had been submitted by the Landlord's agents and rejected.

[Facility]: The Landlord's agents had reduced their figure for the reviewed rent to £13,500. Negotiations continue.

b) The sale of [facility] was proceeding with exchange of contracts expected for mid-February and completion by 1st April. It was noted that receipt of the sale monies had not been built into the cash flow forecast and that if this sale completed as anticipated the additional overdraft facility would not be needed.

c) The possibility of selling the business and licensing or underletting the lease at [facility] was being pursued urgently.

d) Insurance: The Secretary would draft a letter to go to Landlords requesting that the interest of the company be noted on the insurance policy to ensure any liability in the event of loss was minimised.

Action: JKL

7. Sealing

The Secretary produced Register of Seals to the Board and approval was granted to the affixing of the company seal to items numbered 345 to 357 and 359 to 361, and approval granted to the signing as a deed of item 378. The Chairman was authorised to sign the register in evidence of this approval, and did so. (13)

8. Board Meeting timetable

The dates of the meetings of the Board for the second half of the following calendar year (dates for the first half remaining unchanged) were confirmed as 28th July, 24th August, 23rd September, 26th October, 23rd November, and 21st December.

The Secretary was requested to inform Mr UVW of these dates as soon as possible. (14)

Chairman .... 23rd December 1998 (15)

Notes:

1. Pages of Board Meeting Minutes should be consecutively numbered (particularly if a loose-leaf binder is used). The subject of each minute (where applicable) should be indexed and a degree of cross-referencing provided.

2. Stating the exact length of attendance of advisors, and even of members if they do not stay for the whole meeting, is advisable.

3. It is also advisable for Directors to sign an attendance book.

4. Ideally the Chairman should initial each page of the Minutes of each meeting except for the last which should be signed. See 15 below.

5. Placing the initials of the person due to deal with the item enables the Minutes (already a document of record and reference) to act also as a means of encouraging action.

6. Depending upon the requirements of the Articles it is important that any Director with an interest in the subject matter declares that interest.

7. Framing a decision in this way leaves some leeway for delay should the circumstances at the time warrant such delay.

8. Where a lengthy document is required to be approved, rather than repeating the whole item in the Minutes, copying it and attaching it to the Minutes is advisable. It should then be numbered either consecutively after the last page number for that meeting, or take the number of the past page and 'a' 'b' 'c' etc., added with a designatory letter for each page of the item. Banks may wish to have a set form of resolution adopted for the approval of their mandate and similar business.

9. Reference should be made to the Articles to ensure the Board are acting in accordance with them.

10. In the event that any Director wishes his/her dissent to be recorded this must occur although often the Chairman will seek to avoid or minimise the inclusion of such a comment.

11. Ideally all Directors should be present for the whole meeting but if this is not possible, the time that a Director arrived/left should be noted.

12. To save the time of the meeting, it may be possible to distribute a report (as here) with the agenda and simply report on any update since the date of the agenda.

13. Although not a statutory requirement, the use of a Register of Seals and subsequent approval of all entries provides Board authority for the items. It also enables details of items signed as deeds, where the use of the seal has been dispensed, with to be noted. The Chairman should sign under the last number authorised at the meeting and should add the date. Ideally the number of each seal entry in the Register should appear on the item sealed as a further cross-reference of authority.

14. When meetings are arranged in the absence of a colleague, these may clash with other commitments already entered into. Early advice of the dates is essential. Ideally the dates of Board Meetings should be arranged on a rolling 18 month basis. With the immediate six months date firm, the following six months subject to some leeway and the third six months indicative only.

15. Inserting a place for the Chairman to sign and adding the date (of the next planned meeting) emphasises the importance of signing as well as making the Minutes themselves appear better presented.

Note: Some companies number each minute consecutively, starting from 1 at the beginning of the financial or calendar year. This may aid cross-referencing.

Summary checklist

✓ Board members must have sufficient time and data to prepare individually for meetings and to check data submitted.

✓ Reports need to be prepared concisely and effectively and ideally in a standard format.

✓ Where 'pet' business is to be transacted, principles of negotiation and/or power play with colleagues need to be addressed.

✓ Business decisions need to be recorded accurately in Minutes which are not only vital records of business but also can be used to progress chase.

7

chapter seven

A meeting's two key players

The Chairman and the Secretary

Key players

Whilst every meeting is different and every requirement varies, there are two key players common to most meetings: A Chairman and a Secretary – someone to lead the discussion and ensure the meeting makes the required decisions, and someone to take notes of the decisions arrived at. Effective meetings need both and as key players their joint and separate impact on the meeting can be considerable.

General responsibilities of the Chairman

The position of the Chairman is pivotal in terms of the effectiveness of the meeting and its approach to and determination of its work. One of any Chairman's prime tasks should be to drive the company forward which may mean ensuring that the Board needs to be posed with strategical questions and a requirement to formulate at least medium-term plans, rather than concentrating on results which are often 'past news' before they are considered. The meeting will normally reflect far more the character, drive and inspiration of the Chairman than any other factor or member. If this is not so then it may be that the meeting is being dominated by someone other than the Chairman. The Chairman should be able to lead by force of personality and respect.

Chairman's general responsibilities

a) To ensure that each meeting is geared to moving the company forward to the aims set for it and to attain the plans set by the meeting itself.

b) To take responsibility for pushing the meeting itself to consider all its business (including forward planning) and to attain its aims.

c) To be conscious of what is trying to be achieved from each item of business and from the entire meeting.

d) To ensure that not only is each item on the agenda dealt with comprehensively, but also that all members are heard on the subject, which may mean actively inviting members to contribute, rather than passively waiting for them to do so.

e) To ensure that members act and deliberate as Directors of the whole company rather than as managers of their particular function.

f) To bring the meeting back to the business in hand should it stray from such considerations.

g) To close down members' arguments of contentions where these threaten to detract from proper consideration of the subject matter and are not progressing the discussion. This is particularly relevant if the meeting is subject to a time limit. The problem is that often the value of such contributions may be in inverse proportion to the amount of time spent propounding them. Moving the meeting on can then take a great deal of tact.

h) To ensure the decisions arrived at are recorded and promulgated and subsequent meetings are arranged only when business requires.

i) To lead the discussion and the meeting itself. A Chairman is a leader and an effective leader is someone who makes things happen and achieves results through people. The required work of the Chairman is thus to make things happen.

An effective Chairman will have determined the purpose of the meeting, and will wish to see the items of business considered by the meeting moved towards the attainment of the purpose. If he becomes aware of any possibility of this aim being frustrated, it is his responsibility to try to 'take out' or 'neutralise' the opposition. Since this may be difficult in the meeting itself, as it will gain attention and the opposition might gain support, it may be best for him to take the initiative in advance of the meeting.

Constructive diversion

The Chairman became aware that a Board member intended raising the question of standards of on-site safety at the Board. He was also aware that the Director responsible was under great pressure and were such an emotive matter to be raised in public forum, a divisive argument was certain to develop. Accordingly, he set up an informal discussion in advance of the Board Meeting to consider how safety standards could be improved. In such a neutral atmosphere and under duress from the Chairman, a joint approach using the skills of both parties in harmony was developed. The Board simply received a brief verbal report of the initiative.

Key technique:

In this instance the Chairman was made aware of the development by the Secretary who acted as his confidante and shop floor 'ears and eyes'. As an alternative the Chairman needs a high profile presence so that he becomes aware personally of the developments, or has sufficient perception to second guess them. However, by virtue of his position it may be difficult for him to receive such messages – few may be prepared to reveal the true state of affairs.

Progressing the meeting

Chairmanship relies on a strong personality, to carry both business and members along, and in order to manipulate the meeting so that its aims are achieved. The Chairman needs to have:

- Vision, to move the meeting towards the attainment of its aims

- Perception so that almost by instinct and certainly from a process of sound leadership and active listening (see Chapter 10) he is aware of the aspirations and preferences of each member

- Good communication skills so that this vision is easily communicated to the other meeting members

- Enthusiasm to motivate members so that they learn to believe in plans and in their own ability to perform and achieve them

- The ability to delegate, to force decision making and accountability down the chain of command, not so that someone at a low level can be left 'carrying the can' but to widen their horizons, make them aware of the issues and encourage them to make suggestions, and

- An awareness that from time to time certain Board members may need support and be prepared to provide this.

Boards are at their most effective when they act as a team under a dynamic leader. Individual disagreements need to be sublimated in favour of a common concerted approach.

Laying on the line

c*a*se

The Chairman in his opening address to the new divisional Board, not only welcomed all members but stated that the Board would be run as informally as possible, but that this would be matched by a need for total accountability and commitment. He added that he only wanted members at the meeting who were prepared to operate under those guidelines and invited anyone not prepared to do so to leave the meeting. No-one moved.

Controlling and motivating

Key technique:

This public declaration acted as considerable peer pressure on all present.

Controlling the members

Effective meetings may require the Chairman to manipulate the members as well as the meeting, which may not be as difficult or Machiavellian as it sounds, since if people can identify with a successful effort they tend to co-operate and work more effectively in most cases. If they have something of which they can be proud, and know that their contribution is important to the meeting and the organisation, they tend to commit to a far greater degree than is otherwise the case. In any event, basic involvement tends to create an environment where individuals work willingly. What is needed is for the Chairman to motivate the members, for example, by the judicious use of praise, and by allowing them to bring to the meeting certain problems for discussion and assistance. Even though such business may be outside the strict aims of the meeting, allowing such discussion should engender a positive attitude. Within an established meeting consensus may often be achieved, although there may be instances when conflict will surface. Indeed it is arguable that a certain amount of constructive conflict can generate ideas and move the meeting towards its aims. If destructive conflict arises, the Chairman needs to be able to either remove it or direct it positively.

Motivating members

The role of Chairman combines that of 'first among equals' with that of leader, and this dual role should always be recognised. In the latter endeavour the Chairman should ensure the best of each member is brought out. Unfortunately it can be easy for a dominant person to take over the meeting and for less dominant members to be overshadowed to such an extent that they make little or no contribution. If this occurs then the Chairman's responsibility is to encourage the quieter members to make a contribution, even, if necessary, silencing others in order to allow them to do so. In this the Chairman may find it helpful to adopt the following guidelines:

Motivating members

1. Ensure everyone knows why they are present. In this he may need to restate the meetings objectives. He may also state the time within which he would like to see the business conducted. Such strictures must be promoted positively, the aim being to complete the business properly, recognising that time is scarce and valuable.

2. Treat every member as an individual with rights to make the points they wish. This may require the Chairman inviting a contribution by name from 'less forward' member(s).

3. Encourage every member to identify with the body as a whole and to relate to every other member. This will take time and, with some members, can be difficult.

4. Encourage a sense of pride in the meeting and its achievements. Without being excessive, the Chairman should praise achievements whether these be joint or individual. As a nation we in the UK tend to criticise too much and praise too little, even though praise (which costs nothing) can be the most powerful motivator and incentive. It is also helpful when trying to manipulate a meeting, since this 'feel good' effect can stifle or neutralise what could otherwise be objections.

5. Ensure all members are treated fairly and given a chance both to explain their views and attitudes and

to argue their cases. Obviously this in turn requires the opposition to have a chance to do the same. If members see that each is allowed his own turn to put forward arguments, the temptation to filibuster or use other means by which the arguments of others are not heard should be reduced.

6. Ensure members feel that business which they feel is important does receive the attention it deserves. This may be difficult in the early life of a meeting and the Chairman needs to be tactful in accepting or rejecting business requested by members. If it is entirely germane to the business in hand, it may be worth considering, even if that in turn means the meeting overruns its allotted time span. If it is not appropriate, a tactful suggestion 'perhaps we could have an initial chat about that after the meeting' might solve the problem without disincentivising the member.

Dealing with opposition

Whilst most business and most Boards operate with mutual respect and consensus, from time to time opposition may arise which, despite prior attempted pre-emption, may surface at a Board Meeting. This will need careful handling by the Chairman although having some advance notice of a potential problem may assist. If determined opposition is expected then the meeting should be seated perhaps more informally than usual. Seating everyone in comfortable chairs may reduce the capacity for opposition. This may also provide an opportunity for the dispersal of those who are likely to oppose. This does not mean banishing them to the far corners of the discussion table as this may enable them to regroup and even solicit support from uncommitted members. If there are three people who seek to oppose, then at least one, preferably the leader, should be seated very near the Chairman which may enable the latter to control him. If the meeting uses the principle of the House of Commons, where before speaking a member has to catch the Speaker's eye, so that to speak the Chairman has to grant permission, even if only by the briefest of nods then the person located nearest the Chairman will then have the greatest difficult, by sheer juxtaposition, in catching his close neighbour's eye!

Other opposition members need to be spread amongst supporters of the Chairman. In this way, their apparent strength or weight will be marginalised, they will find it difficult to communicate between themselves, which may be necessary in order to re-group or seek an alternative tactic. In addition, if they are each seated next to a strong supporter of the business, the opposition may feel inhibited about making their protest at all, or continuing it in the face of experienced or heavy opposition. The layout set out overleaf shows how opposition groups can be split and to some extent neutralised.

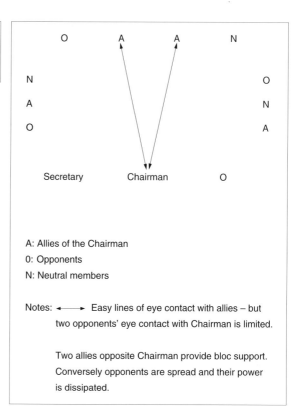

A: Allies of the Chairman
0: Opponents
N: Neutral members

Notes: ◄────► Easy lines of eye contact with allies – but
two opponents' eye contact with Chairman is limited.

Two allies opposite Chairman provide bloc support.
Conversely opponents are spread and their power
is dissipated.

Seating plan negating opposition 'blocs'
(from *Manipulating Meetings*, David Martin)

Silencing the opposition

As well as physically splitting the opposition, the Chairman
has power to downgrade their contribution by:

- 'Not seeing' that they wish to make a contribution
  and thus not inviting their input

- 'Cutting across' their contribution should they stray
  for one moment from the core of the subject

- Applying 'kangaroo' or 'closure' motions, (i.e. restricting
  comments and arguments and discussion of the
  whole to a short period).

In addition the Chairman can allow dissenters too much time so that they start repeating themselves. Allowing too much time can imply that what has been said has not been very telling and it is assumed that they have further points to make. If none can be made, the inference is then of an unfinished and possibly insufficiently supported case. Conversely, in allowing a right of reply, the Chairman may allow a supporter more time 'by mistake' to try and counter the case, although advance briefing of this possibility may be necessary.

Should the situation develop where a project thought to be essential for the business is likely to fail, due to the activities of the opposition despite all the steps taken to negate their impact, the Chairman may need to act swiftly to ensure its survival, if not at the current meeting, then at an adjournment or subsequent meeting. In such a situation, the Chairman, anticipating outvoting and defeat may need either to withdraw the item, to propose that it 'be left on the table', that is held over until the following meeting, or to adjourn the meeting itself. His powers to perform any or all of these acts will depend on the terms of reference of the meeting and the support of the members. It is essential that the Chairman knows his terms of reference, the delineation of all his powers and his likely support.

The role of the Company Secretary

Good secretaryship, like good administration, tends not to be seen but to play its part with quiet efficiency. This tends to underplay the vital importance of the role of the Company Secretary as:

- Guardian, ensuring fulfilment of the company's obligation to comply with legislation

- Facilitator, easing communication between the Board and management

- Confidante, supporting all members of the Board and particularly the Chairman, and

- Chief administrative officer of the company (including being a legal 'officer' of the company with all the attendant responsibilities and liabilities that description entails – Section 744 Companies Act 1985).

In 1971 the then Master of the Rolls, Lord Denning defined the Secretary as 'the chief administrative officer of the company – he regularly makes representations on behalf of the company and enters into contracts on its behalf. He is entitled to sign contracts – all such matters come within the ostensible authority of the Company Secretary'. Since then the role has gained an increasing prominence – likely to be further enhanced by new initiatives in company compliance.

To a large extent the importance of the role is determined by the fact that unlike Directors, there are restrictions on those who are able to be appointed Company Secretary in the Companies Act 1985 – at least for PLCs. Effectively, unless there are very strong reasons for ignoring the requirements, a PLC Company Secretary must hold a professional qualification.

Writing in the '*Chartered Secretary*' (the journal of the Chartered Institute of Secretaries) former Chief Executive of ICI, Sir John Harvey-Jones commented 'the Company Secretary is an absolutely key appointment – more important than that of any Director' and went on to describe the role as 'creative'. In Sir John's view, 'the Company Secretary needs to be dynamic'.

In some companies, in his relationship with meetings, a good Secretary, like Victorian children, may be required to be seen and not heard, only supporting the meeting administratively. But this somewhat restricted view of the role, may be shortsighted as the Secretary will often have a more comprehensive view of the business under discussion than some members and certainly has an obligation to be fully aware of all legal obligations. To quote Sir John again 'I always work with a positive Board system, by which I mean I don't allow silence. After discussing each subject I ask each member of the Board what their opinion is and why – this includes the Company Secretary as I have always believed that his view should be heard'. The views of the Company Secretary may be more objective than that of Directors some of whom may, despite their Board responsibilities, be more interested in 'fighting the corner' for their own executive responsibilities.

The Cadbury Committee on Corporate Governance recognised the unique position of the Company Secretary stating 'the Company Secretary has a key role to play in ensuring that the Board procedures are followed and regularly reviewed. The Chairman and the Board will look to the Company Secretary for guidance on what their responsibilities are'.

The Cadbury report also suggested that all Directors (and this would apply particularly to non-executive Directors which it regarded as having views that were independent from and potentially more objective than, executive Directors) should always have access to the Company Secretary and that any suggestion of the dismissal or removal of the Company Secretary should be considered by the whole Board.

It is one of the responsibilities of the Board to appoint a suitable and capable Company Secretary and to ensure that the appointee maintains these attributes. In many ways this is his most onerous task since the impact of legislation on companies from many areas is immense and continues to grow and a prime responsibility of the Company Secretary should be to 'keep the company legal.'

Responsibilities

There are well over a million companies and no doubt a million different job descriptions for their Company Secretaries. In the checklist below is set out the main responsibilities of most Company Secretaries but this needs to be individually customised. It is a prime responsibility of the Board to ensure these duties are carried out.

Main duties of the Company Secretary

a) Understand and interpret the requirements and obligations contained in the Memorandum and Articles and guide the Board on these.

b) Maintain statutory registers. This entails updating and keeping updated the various statutory books including the register of members which involves transferring shares, issuing new certificates etc. although many companies with large numbers of shareholders delegate such work to specialised divisions of, for example, the clearing banks.

c) Update Registrar of Companies. The Secretary is responsible for advising the Registrar promptly of all changes in Directorate, of all charges over assets, of changes in shareholders at least once a year, etc. and other matters affecting the corporate nature of the company.

d) Ensure compliance with Company Law. The Secretary must have a good working knowledge of the require-ments placed upon the Directors under Company Law and ensure that the company complies with such requirements and all changes and innovations.

e) Liaise with shareholders. The extent of this respon-sibility will depend on the individual companies – in some, the Directors take on this role, however, in most the Secretary is responsible for at least the documentary contact with shareholders – i.e. notice of meeting, preparation of Annual Report etc.

f) Ensure legally required documentation is prepared. This is a very wide-ranging responsibility since much of what is required is derived from obligations under commercial, employment and other laws and familiarity with such laws and obligations is essential.

g) Convene company and Board Meetings. The Secretary can only do this at the direction of the Board but to ensure the Board fulfils its own duties he needs to ensure that Board Meetings are held regularly – compile Minutes of meetings and subcommittees. This is an onerous but essential part of his duties not simply to preserve the record of control, but also to have available documentary evidence which might be needed as a defence in any actions against Directors.

h) File accounts and annual return. Increasingly the obligation to file such items within specified time limits is being backed by rigorously enforced fines. Repeated failure to file on time can lead to disqualification from office.

i) Carry out instructions of Board. As the chief administrative officer of the company, the Secretary may have the prime role for interfacing with management. Alternatively, executive Directors may take this role – whoever takes it needs to comply with the exact requirements of the Board.

j) (For PLC only) Liaise with the Stock Exchange and ensure the requirements of the Listing Agreement are complied with.

k) Act as Board/Chairman's confidante. This is often one of the roles played by the Secretary particularly where he is not also a Director as he can bring an objective view to the work of the Board. It is also often possible for the Secretary to be aware of internal developments of which Directors are not aware and thus provide a valuable communication conduit to the Chairman.

l) Act as chief administrative officer. The scope for this responsibility will vary from company to company, nevertheless the Secretary is often the source from which management first learn of and are required to implement decisions

m) Protect the company's assets. It is the Secretary's duty to protect the statutory books and records of the company and the confidentiality of the Board's work. It may be logical to make him responsible for other aspects of corporate security.

n) Ensure all proper returns are made (and in time). The officers of the company, of which the Secretary is one, have an obligation to comply with the filing regulations of Company Law. If these are not filed by the due date, fines can be levied, repetition of which could lead to disqualification.

o) Oversee legal matters. Often the Secretary is legally qualified or will be the only executive with some experience of the law. Increasingly the law is intruding on company activities and someone must assume this responsibility.

p) Oversee the arrangements to allow shareholders and others to inspect certain records of the company and to provide access to statutory and other bodies to inspect other records.

q) Ensure compliance

- Contractual and commercial law

- Health and Safety law

- Environmental law

- Employment law.

This is so vast an obligation it is difficult to visualise how a working Secretary with the usual range of additional duties can hope to provide advice and guidance on such matters. It is expected that the new Companies Act will place further responsibilities for compliance on the Company Secretary which could force companies to provide additional funding to enable this compliance obligation to be addressed suitably. Unless this is done a Secretary may be able to escape liability for acts or negligence simply by claiming that sufficient funds to enable him to do the job properly were not made available. As if the foregoing range of requirements were not wide itself many Company Secretaries will also take responsibility for insurance, pensions, property, security and even employment and/or financial matters.

Before and at Board Meetings

Much of the Secretary's work will revolve around convening, servicing and administering Board Meetings. His respon-sibilities in this work are summarised in the checklist below but inevitably particular companies will have different requirements. Directors have an obligation to ensure that this work is carried out appropriately bearing in mind that Board Meetings and the Minutes thereof provide evidence of the reasons for and the decisions taken by the Board.

The Secretary's responsibility for Board Meetings

a) Generating an agenda in liaison with the Chairman (see Chapter 5 re the value of a dynamic agenda).

b) Ensuring all data for consideration by the Board accompanies the agenda or there is a date by which it will be ready and distributed. Accompanying data should be presented in the order in which it will be considered on the agenda.

c) Convening the meeting in good time. There is no legal requirement regarding notice due to be given of a Board Meeting but for commercial reasons and to allow the Directors to be properly briefed at least seven days notice with required data should be given. It would also be logical for the Secretary to take responsibility for compiling and updating a timetable of future meetings.

d) Ensuring, if a quorum is required to be present before the meeting can commence, that at least members satisfying that requirement are to be present to avoid wasting the time of others attending.

e) Taking, reporting and recording any apologies for absence and noting any late arrivals or early departures so that it can be shown who was present when any decision was taken.

f) Having available any statutory and other registers that need to be inspected and/or signed (e.g. the Registers of Seals, Director's interests, etc.)

g) Checking members have all the documents required but having available spare documents in case members have mislaid or forgotten them.

h) Ensuring meetings supports, provision of refreshments, note taking aids, protection against interruption, and so on, are in operation.

i) Ensuring meeting adheres to and does not overlook any item on the agenda.

j) Ensuring those who speak and vote are entitled to do so.

k) Ensuring the meeting does take required decisions and that these are clear and clearly understood by all present.

l) Noting the sense of the meeting in the Minutes.

m) Preparing Minutes, having them approved in draft by the Chairman, distributed to the members and approved by them at their next following meeting.

n) Keeping the Minutes secure and available to members of the Board and the auditors.

o) Ensuring action is effected as required by the meeting and reported on at the appropriate time.

p) Anticipating the level of support available, and any antipathy or opposition to, matters due to be considered by the Board and briefing the Chairman accordingly.

q) Being proactive in all respects.

and so on.

Summary checklist

✓ The duties and responsibilities of the Chairman in forcing the work of the Board should be delineated and promulgated to all.

✓ The Chairman must take responsibility for pushing the meeting to achieve its purposes (and the company its aims).

✓ The Chairman must also take responsibility for controlling and motivating Board members and ensuring the positive outcome of Board business.

✓ The Board must delineate the responsibilities of the Company Secretary and ensure these are carried out. The Secretary must be proactive in ensuring legal compliance and internal administration as a result thereof.

chapter eight

An inspector calls

Access, authorities and auditors

General requirements to protect records

Protections and inspections

The officers of a company have a general duty to preserve and protect the statutory and other records of the company – not least the financial records and there are severe penalties for failing to do so. In addition, included in the duties of the Board in general and the Company Secretary in particular should be the obligation to arrange for the inspection of the company records by those entitled – an obligation often overlooked. A short time ago a national newspaper bought a few shares in each of a number of leading listed PLCs and sought to exercise the right of inspection of the statutory books as a shareholder. It sent a representative to the registered offices, but the answers the enquiries received were many and varied and in several cases totally in breach of Company Law. One leading company refused to produce the Directors' service contracts, another tried to defer the inspection for a month whilst a Director of a third company commented 'I'm far too busy running the company to bother about things like that'. Whilst hard-pressed Directors and Secretaries may have some sympathy with the last comment it is still an illegal response and reflects poorly on the professionalism of the companies. Since each company was in the top 100 one would expect their officers to know the law and be the first to comply.

Access to and inspection of records can be regarded under two headings:

a) The rights of access of shareholders and others to inspect the statutory books of the company (see the checklist overleaf) and

b) The rights of access and inspection of these and other records by a variety of other statutory bodies and those with whom the company has contractual relationships (see the checklist on page 150).

Statutory records inspection

Shareholders own the company and the records of the company technically and legally belong to them. For two hours every business day, shareholders have the right of access to these statutory records. In addition they may take such copies as they wish, although if the company provides copying facilities (which it is not obliged to do) it can charge the rates prescribed for such copies. Creditors and members of the public can also inspect some of these records – and again the records must be held open for two hours each day for them.

Rights of access to statutory records

The following have rights of access to the records stated:

a) The company's creditors: Free access to the Register of Charges and any statutory declaration of payment out of capital for redemption or purchase of its own shares.

b) The public: To items under a) above (for which an access charge of not more than 5p can be made) PLUS the Registers of Members, Overseas Branch, Directors & Secretary, Directors' interests, Significant shareholdings (PLC only), and Debenture holders; reports on disclosure of holders under section 212 and contract(s) for purchase by company of its own shares. A charge of £2.50 per hour can be made.

c) The company shareholders: Free access to items under a) and b) above plus Register of Transactions not disclosed in accounts (e.g. Director's loans) and Directors' service contracts.

External authorities

As well as the rights of access of shareholders, creditors and the public to the statutory records, a seemingly ever-increasing number of bodies also have rights of access to both the company premises as well as its records and, again, if the company is not to be seen as acting unprofessionally as well as illegally, Directors should make arrangements for, and brief their staff in, the administration of such visits.

Rights of access of authorities and parties to contracts

Policy

1. Representatives of the following organisations have a right of access to company premises, have rights (brief details as shown below for each) to inspect records and interview employees and may also have a right to remove records, data and registers etc.

2. The receptionist/gate keeper on duty should establish the agency the visitor(s) represent and inspect their credentials to ensure their bona fides. (S)he should conduct them to the waiting room and contact the company representative stated who will be responsible for dealing with the enquiry.

3. Agencies with right of access, company contact and initial action:

   a) Department of Trade and Industry (DTI), Self-Regulatory Organisations (SRO), Serious Fraud Office (SFO), Office of Fair Trading (OFT), European Union (EU) Inspectorate.

   Contact: Company Secretary (whom failing Assistant Company Secretary, whom failing Chief Accountant).

   Action: Telephone corporate lawyers to interface, telephone public relations firm to brief them in case media require information and/or to prepare a press statement, advise Chairman and Board. Meet representatives and endeavour to ascertain requirements. Check requirements with corporate lawyers. Endeavour to assist investigators whilst indicating the potential damage to the company name and reputation. Write report of visit, requirements, action carried out, records inspected/removed, and so on.

Note: Representatives of some of these organisations have a right of immediate access, to seize documents and to demand statements from personnel (who do not have, on pain of penalty, a right of silence) – immediate legal advice is essential.

b) Inland Revenue (IR), Department of Social Security (DSS), Customs and Excise (C&E), Occupational Pensions Regulator, Data Protection Registrar, Rating Authorities.

Contact: Chief Accountant (whom failing Finance Director, whom failing Company Secretary).

Action: Meet representatives and establish nature of enquiry – provide information required. Advise Chairman and Board and corporate lawyers (via Company Secretary). Ensure, if errors are found that systems are changed to avoid a repetition. Discipline staff if procedures have not been followed correctly. Write report of visit, action required and effected, and so on.

c) Fire, Police, Factory Inspectorate, Gas, Water and Electricity utilities, Minimum wage inspectors.

Contact: Personnel Director (whom failing Company Secretary, whom failing Personnel Manager).

Action: Meet representative and establish problem. Rectify if required and possible. Update procedures if required. Write report of visit and action effected.

d) Environmental Health, Trading Standards.

Contact: Retail Director (whom failing Personnel Director, whom failing Company Secretary).

Action: Meet representative and establish problem. Rectify if required and possible. Update procedures if required. Write report of visit and action effected.

e) Department of Transport.

Contact: Transport Manager (whom failing Company Secretary).

Action: Be prepared to produce operators licence and back-up records (e.g. plating records etc.).

f) Landlord and agents.

Contact: Company Secretary (whom failing Assistant Company Secretary, whom failing Chief Accountant).

Action: Meet representatives – since most leases state that (say) 48 hours notice of such an inspection must be given there will be no need to allow immediate access unless it is an emergency. Good landlord/tenant relations may require a positive and helpful approach. Note requirements. If a dilapidations notice (a schedule of 'wants of repair' that have arisen because the repairing obligations of the lease have not been complied with) is to be served, refer to the lease for the procedure to be followed.

Details of aims of and data likely to be required by bodies requiring access:

DTI – to investigate company affairs, ownership, dealings in shares including insider dealing. Exact nature of investigation needs to be ascertained.

SRO – the various self-regulatory bodies have powers under the Financial Services Act to investigate the affairs of their members.

SFO – the Serious Fraud Office has powers, wider in many cases than those available to the police or SROs, to investigate matters of fraud likely to total in excess of £2 million and to be of public concern.

IR & DSS – the powers of access tend to be exercised by their audit departments and compliance units, charged with the duty of checking the validity of the way an employer has deducted tax and NI from his employees and paid it over to the Revenue. The Inland Revenue also oversees the assessment of properties for commercial rating purposes.

C&E – have wide powers of access in respect of their VAT collection duties which emanate from their old role as excise officers. The penalties for, even totally accidental, errors, in VAT collection and payment are severe although currently under review.

OFT – the Office of Fair Trading has an obligation to investigate whether supplies of goods or services breach the principles of the Fair Trading Act 1973 and/or the Competition Act 1980 – i.e. whether control of a market is such that a reference should be made to the Mergers and Monopolies Commission.

EU – inspectors have rights to enter the premises of organisations of member states under EU law although it has been stated that, in doing so they should try to act in accordance with the laws of the member state concerned (and via domestic authorities).

Occupational Pensions Regulator – has a right of access to inspect pension records under the Pensions Act 1995 and a right to apply for a warrant to search premises for purposes connected with compliance with the requirements.

Inspectors concerned with minimum wage application – will presumably have a right of access to check that the requirements of the minimum wage are being complied with.

Data Protection registrar – will have a right of access under the 1998 revision/extension of Data Protection legislation.

Fire – the local Fire Officer has a right of access to premises mainly for the purposes of checking compliance with fire certificate and fire regulations matters, and requirements regarding fire safety previously made by him – or required under statute to be carried out by the occupier and/or owner.

Police – unless in the belief, or in connection with such belief, that a crime is about to, or is being committed, or in 'hot pursuit' of a suspected person, or to prevent a breach of the peace, the police have no immediate right of access to premises other than with the permission of the owner.

Health and Safety Executive, Environmental Health Officers, Factory Inspectors – have a range of powers which vary from industry to industry. Operators of large (and potential hazardous) facilities are obliged (under the Control of Industrial Major Accident Regulations 1988) to file and keep up to date details of plans and emergency evacuations etc. which will require an interface with the appropriate department which may well wish to check the site.

Dept of Transport – have rights to inspect transport operators licence and administration.

Local Authorities – have an increasing range of obligations – particularly under the Food Safety and Environment Protection Acts.

Rating Officers (a) and Trading Standards Officers (b) need access to check details of the establishment (a) for the purpose of assessment to the Uniform Business Rate, and (b) to ensure compliance with the relevant trading laws.

Gas, Water, Electricity utilities – access to read meters and, if leaks/breaks are suspected or, in the event of emergencies, to rectify.

Landlord and agents – to inspect condition and use of premises, assess value for insurance, prepare dilapidations reports, erect letting signs at end of lease etc.

In addition to the above list, further bodies have powers of access for particular industries. These should be established and their details, sphere of authority and action required added to the list. For example interested parties (which could include members of the public) have a right to inspect Safety Plans drawn up in compliance with the Construction (Design and Management) Regulations 1994 relating to building works.

Control

Another prime responsibility of the officers (not only to provide adequate financial controls but also to attempt to protect their own position) is to ensure that:

a) Control for the acts of the company are taken in accordance with agreed procedures, and

b) All commitments are entered into by (and only by) properly authorised persons. The company can be held liable for the acts of its employees who will often be deemed to be acting as its agents or in the course of their employment (even if such actions would not normally be considered as such or authorised by the Board – see résumé of decisions of cases in Chapter 3). Directors need to ensure that employees are aware of the manner and scope of their action – and that such rules are actively policed and breaches made subject to appropriate sanctions.

Minimising liability –
a checklist for employers

Ensure that

1. All rules regarding trading, outlawing price-fixing, safety, recruitment as well as attitudes and actions towards employees during employment regarding respect and fair treatment are clear and adhered to at all times.

2. All employees have read and understood the rules and all procedures etc., are regularly checked and policed and always adhered to (without exception).

3. Immediate action is taken if there is any question of an accusation or suspicion that there is a breach of such rules and that sanctions are effected against those in breach.

4. All safety rules are adhered to, specifications regarding maintenance are compiled with and inspections are carried out in accordance therewith.

5. All reports of problems affecting or potentially affecting safety are dealt with immediately.

6. All employees are advised of their responsibilities for their own, their colleagues', and their employers assets' safety.

7. Everyone is constantly reminded of the need to adhere to rules, procedures etc., to think before acting or speaking and to consider the implications of liability claims.

8. The company rules and procedures are:

   • Codified and user-friendly

   • Regularly updated and promulgated

   • Always adhered to, and that

   • Employees can be shown to have knowledge of them.

Controlling exercise of authority

Commitment authority

It is essential for the proper control of the monetary and other assets of the company, that authority is granted at, and only at, the appropriate level in order to incur expenditure or approve the disposal of stocks (and any other assets) other than in the normal course of trade. Since the officers could be held to be liable to third parties when liabilities have been created due to approval being given at a level which had no authority to grant such approval, there is a strong incentive as well as a commercial validity in publishing, updating and ensuring adherence to a schedule of authority such as the draft set out in the example below. Most auditors will welcome the use of such a schedule as it should assist them in checking that approval was given at an appropriate level and by an authorised person to all transactions. Further the development and policing of authorities' control can be an effective means of minimising fraud.

Authority chart

BUSINESS NAME   AUTHORITY LEVELS

Philosophy: It is essential for the proper control of the company that approval is granted to contracts by suitably appointed personnel and, for the allocation and disposal of money and stock assets of the organisation, that authority is granted at an appropriate level.

Contracts

All contracts between the company and third parties, other than those covered by items specifically set out below, must be channelled through the Company Secretary's office, to ensure correct status (i.e. whether it is to be regarded as a Deed or not) and approval.

For a document to be sealed or signed as a deed at least two weeks notice of the effective date of approval should be given and, should it consist of more than [say, five pages] a synopsis should be provided.

The Company Secretary will arrange the passing of suitable Board resolutions granting approval to specified person(s) to sign on behalf of the company. It should be noted that sufficient time (specify requirement) to obtain such a resolution should be allowed.

Contracts of employment for those earning in excess of [sum] must be signed on behalf of the company by [name]. Contracts for those earning less than this sum must be signed by [name].

Cash commitment   *Authority levels*

Capital projects:

Authority for all projects
(Note: No minimum threshold)   Board

(All items must be supported by a
Capital Expenditure (Capex) Form

Repairs and renewals, purchase of furniture and fittings
(All items must be supported by a Capex form)

Up to £1000   Manager – level…

Over £1000 and up to £5000   Director

Over £5000   Board

Vehicles
(Supported by Capex Form, for new allocations, or
Replacement Form (for write-offs and replacements)

                                                             Board

All purchases to be in accordance with Policy

Expense items
Up to £500   Manager – level…

Over £500 and up to £1000   Senior Manager

Over £1000 and up to £5000   Director

Over £5000   Board

Committed expenditure

Rent, rates, utility costs – where no change or increase is less than rate of inflation	Manager – level…
Where change has taken place	Director

Bought ledger

Raw materials, services etc., in accordance with budgeted level of production	Purchasing Manager
Not in accordance with level of production	Director

Personnel

Wage adjustments

Annual Review	Board
Other than annual review, or for new staff, or replacement at other than at old rate	
Salary up to £10,000 p.a.	Manager – level…
Salary over £10,000 p.a.	Board

Discipline

Warnings (verbal)	Manager – level…
Warnings (written – grades [x] to [y])	Director
(written – other grades)	Manager – level…
Dismissal	Director

Sundry transactions

Credits (cash or stock), samples, etc. In accordance with policy and less than £1000	Manager – level…
Over £1000	Director
Gifts, donations (cash or stock) in accordance with policy and budget	Personnel Manager

Stock write-off and/or authority to dispose in stated area (e.g. to market trader, staff shop, by gift, etc.)

Up to £1000   Sales Manager

Over £1000   Sales Director in liaison
                                                                             with Finance Director

Expenses

Personal expenses (inc. telephone bills etc.)

Up to £500   By level above level
                                                              submitting the expense claim

Over £500   By level two above person
                                                              submitting expense claim.

                                            (i.e. using the required company form)

Removal expenses

In accordance with range of reimbursement agreed at time may only be authorised by a Board member. All invoices should be submitted in the name of the company to allow recovery of VAT.

Loans

Loans to assist a new employee during the first weeks of his/her employment (i.e. during the working of the 'week in hand' arrangements)   Personnel Manager

All other loans   Board

Issued by Finance Director on (date).

                                            To be updated six monthly.

Directors' loans

The concept of a company making loans to its Directors is anathema to many and this may be a prudent approach since in an age where considerable and adverse attention is given to the rewards that some companies provide for their Directors, such a policy can create an unfortunate impression to many outsiders and even some shareholders. Legally, however, companies are allowed to make the following loans to their Directors:

for PLCs

- Quasi loans of £5000 (repayable within two months)

- Loans to enable the Director to carry out the work of the company of £20,000

- Loans in the ordinary course of business of £100,000.

for LTDs

- Small loans of £5000

- Loans to enable the Director to carry out the work of the company – such figure as is approved by the shareholders

- Loans in the ordinary course of business – to the level that would be allowed to similar but 'unconnected' persons.

Notes:

a) This is a brief résumé of the requirements of the Act which should be referred to for guidance.

b) A quasi loan would exist, for example, if a Director was given a company credit card and allowed to use it for personal expenditure. Until he repaid the company for his personal purchases a 'quasi loan' would exist.

c) The DTI are considering increasing the £5,000 limit to £10,000.

If the details of such loans are not shown in the accounts of the company then such details must be recorded in a Register of Transactions not disclosed in the accounts (section 343, Companies Act 1985) which must be made available for inspection to shareholders for two hours per business day (see page 149).

It would be prudent to ensure that before any loan is made to a Director, the authority of the Board is granted and a note of the fact is made in the Minutes so that the matter is given transparency.

Auditors

Other than the smallest and/or non-trading companies, auditors must be appointed by the shareholders from the incorporation of the company. Although most of their work will be effected with and through the Board (who are usually authorised by the shareholders to agree their fees), Directors should not forget that it is the shareholders who appoint the auditors and it is to the shareholders that the auditors must report. Auditors have a right (indeed a duty) to inspect all aspects of the operation of the business on behalf of their principals (the shareholders) and to report any and all shortcomings. They also need to ensure that the accounts for each financial period (which are the responsibility of the Directors) show a true and fair view of the actual results.

Accordingly the auditors should be:

- Treated with respect by everyone in the company (who should also be briefed on their rights to ask questions of anyone)

- Accorded decent and secure working conditions, and

- Provided with the data they require as swiftly as possible, the demands of the business permitting.

Their investigatory role means that auditors may need to act as a kind of 'critical friend' – appreciating the pressures placed on the Board but ensuring that legal and normal commercial requirements are adhered to. Inevitably at times this means that they can come into conflict with the Directors who may (legitimately or not) have other considerations which force them to a different conclusion or attitude. Such conflicts need to be resolved, but if they cannot and they are of such severity, it may be necessary for the Board to consider recommending that different auditors are appointed.

Whilst there is nothing to stop shareholders and companies changing their auditors, the effect is potentially dangerous and/or damaging to the company's reputation, particularly if the auditors hold views which are supportable in legal and/or financial terms. Auditors have rights should they be required to retire other than with their own agreement. Such agreement would be expected where the proposed retirement is for normal commercial reasons – for example if the company is taken over and the new parent company wishes the audit to be carried out in future by its own auditors. Where auditors do not agree with a request for their retirement, they are entitled to send to the company a statement of any matters which they feel should be submitted to the shareholders. If the Board does not comply with this requirement (i.e. send it to the shareholders within 14 days) or does not alternatively apply to the Court for a dispensation to avoid it notifying the shareholders, the auditor may lodge the statement with the Registrar of Companies who may take action to investigate the position.

If an auditor resigns or is removed then the company must notify the Registrar within 14 days by sending a copy of the resignation statement, or of any resolution removing him as auditor.

To arrange for the appointment of an auditor other than the retiring auditors, special notice is required to be given in the notice of the meeting at which the matter will be considered by the shareholders.

Many auditors perform tasks other than pure auditing for their client companies. They often provide tax advice (and will even calculate any corporation tax payable), management consultancy and even senior recruitment services. Their work interfacing with senior personnel in a variety of companies provides very valuable experience and the insight of many audit partners can be invaluable, particularly when the Board is considering long-term plans. Equally, Directors may find the opportunity of discussing possible new ventures or changes of direction with a senior person, who knows and understands the company well, of considerable benefit.

Summary checklist

✓ Ensure all involved appreciate rights attaching to shareholders and others to inspect statutory books and set up appropriate procedures.

✓ Ensure all involved appreciate rights of statutory and other authorities to have access to the company and its records and set up appropriate procedure for each with guidance as to individual scope.

✓ Restrict ability to commit company and to grant authority to expenditure etc. to those authorities by means of a (regularly updated) Authority Chart.

✓ Loans to Directors must only be made within legal parameters and be properly recorded and disclosed.

✓ Auditors are the custodians of the interests of the shareholders who appoint them. Their legal rights should be known, protected and respected.

chapter nine

Setting an example

Behaviour and approach

Required approach

As a result of the increasing general interest being shown by society in the activities of companies and those that run them, emanating not least from a number of scandals involving well-known companies, their Directors and their advisers, and more positively because generally it is seen to be an indication of sound corporate governance, a large number of leading companies now adopt codes of ethics giving guidance on the level and type of behaviour expected of Directors and senior personnel. Similar codes are available from the Institute of Directors and other professional bodies. The advantage of adopting such codes is that they provide a criteria of expected conduct and in case of doubt can be referred to for guidance – however, all codes are only as effective as those that comply with and those that police them.

Code of ethics/behaviour

1. This company operates under high quality standards – or products, or services and of customer care and requires these standards to be adhered to at all times in all its dealings.

2. No-one working for or employed by, or providing services for the company is to make, or encourage another to make any personal gain out of the activities of the company in any way whatsoever. Any person becoming aware of a personal gain being made so that it offends this clause is required to notify [name] of their suspicion. Provided there are reasonable grounds for such suspicion the position and identity of the person reporting the matter will be protected (see 13 below). Anyone placed in a position where they feel that they could make a personal gain should notify [name] and follow the procedure required.

3. Other than properly authorised trade and retail promotions, no inducement may be offered or given

to any customer or outlet whereby they will be induced or encouraged to place an order for or take any product or service offered by the company.

4. Whilst it is acceptable to entertain a customer to lunch or dinner to discuss normal contractual matters, this must be at places and to the limits laid down in the company's entertainment guide. On no account must the limits and guidelines included in that guide be broken.

5. In the event of any person considering that (s)he needs to entertain or provide a gift for a customer and that the limits are inappropriate (for example the matter concerns an attempt to compensate for previous poor service, quality etc.) the written authority of a member of the Board should be obtained and referred to in the subsequent expenses claim.

6. Employees are allowed to accept hospitality from major customers and suppliers in terms of lunches and/or dinners or other similar value entertainment, to a maximum of [number of occasions] per year. No inducement may be accepted in respect of any third party at any time. In the event that the value obtained is in excess of that laid down in the company entertainment guide, this fact must be made known to a Board member as soon as possible. If the entertainment provided is considered to be in excess of that warranted by the circumstances, the Director responsible may need to contact the third party to explain the policy.

7. Other than at Christmas, employees are not allowed to accept or retain gifts made by any customer or supplier or other third parties, generated because of the business relationship. In the event that such gifts are delivered and it seems potentially damaging to the relationship to return them, then, subject to the approval of [Director] the gifts may be retained and

will be handed to the Social Club for use as raffle prizes or disposed of in a similar way. The Director will contact the donor and explain what has occurred and why.

8. At Christmas, employees are allowed to accept the normal Christmas gifts to a maximum of [amount] per donor. If gifts above this level are received then, subject to the approval of the [Director] they may be retained on the basis set out in 7 above.

9. If multiple Christmas (or other) gifts are received to mark good service received from a number of employees, these may be retained and divided amongst the employees concerned provided the value per employee does not exceed the guidance laid down in the entertainment policy.

10. The attention of all employees is drawn to the danger of a customer or third party using the previous or anticipated delivery of such gifts as a bribe or to exert pressure to obtain concessions (e.g. orders, better terms, preferential treatment) or any other consideration, or using the threat of or actual publicity concerning the acceptance of a gift or lavish entertainment as pressure to obtain concessions etc. In all circumstances the statement 'I cannot comment further – I must contact [Director] to discuss this matter' should be made and the incident reported to [name] immediately.

11. Any suggestion of using facilities owned, occupied or available to a third party (for example a holiday villa or other property, concessionary travel, etc.) either on a free basis or for any consideration which seems or is less than the market price, should be communicated to the [Director] at whose discretion the matter can proceed or be concluded.

12. The company operates with the [specify] industry and is required to and wishes to comply within all

laws, regulations and codes of practice etc. It seeks to trade legally, fairly, openly and honestly with all third parties and to give value for money in all its dealings. It requires and expects its employees to carry out their work and responsibilities and to conduct their relationships and dealings with third parties in accordance with these precepts. All dealings must be conducted openly and fairly in such a way that should every aspect of the transaction become widely known (for example in the media) this would not cause any embarrassment, injury or damage to the reputation of the company whatever.

13. All employees at whatever level in the company are encouraged to report any activities which seem to them to be in breach of this code to [Director]. Such a report will be treated as confidential and provided it is made in good faith and not made with the aim of personal gain, the person making the report should not fear reprisals or detriment.

14. All employees and agents must act responsibly, decently and with due regard for the dignity and rights of others in both business and personal dealings. In many instances personnel (particularly senior personnel) will be seen as acting on behalf of, or by virtue of their position in the company, the reputation of which must be protected at all times.

Note: There will be an increasing likelihood of 'whistleblowing' by employees as a result of the passing of the Public Interest Disclosure Act 1998 aimed at protecting those who report the unacceptable activities of those in their employer's organisations.

Confidentiality undertaking

Where the business, products or plans of an organisation are confidential, either on an ongoing basis or by virtue of developments that occur from time to time, it may be advisable to require those staff likely to be privy to such information to sign a confidentiality undertaking. For public companies subject to the rules regarding the non-disclosure of price-sensitive information this is essential. Merely assuming that those responsible for a breach would be aware of the rules is hardly likely to be an effective defence for any subsequent action.

It is possible for there to be an accidental breach of a confidentiality rule and this needs to be addressed by the organisation. In some ways, acknowledging that accidental breaches can occur and that they will be excluded from the requirements and sanctions set out in the following policy may provide an escape for those deliberately in breach – that is they can try to claim it to be accidental. On the other hand the point that even accidental breach can be subject to sanction helps underline the seriousness of the regard of the employer for the matter.

Ideally the organisation should request signatures to the undertaking to be witnessed. This should avoid the possibility of an employee subject to sanction for breach of the undertaking trying to disclaim knowledge of it by stating that the signature is not theirs and they had not signed such an undertaking.

Draft confidentiality policy

1. The business of the [organisation] entails the development of plans and the production of figures, data and descriptions, all of which are confidential to it and the leakage of which to other parties (or allowing others to become aware of in any way) whether by accident or design is potentially damaging.

2. All employees above [specify grade] are required to sign a confidentiality undertaking.

[For public listed companies only:

All staff of whatever grade who will be involved in the production and recording for publication of information likely to be price-sensitive must on no account divulge such information or give any hint or make any sign or take any action likely to indicate the detail, type or scale of figures or results to a party not privy to such information. Such employees should make themselves aware of the law which seeks to prohibit insider dealing.] (See page 180.)

3. Any member of staff refusing to sign such an undertaking, or proved to be knowingly in breach of such an undertaking having signed it, will be regarded as being guilty of serious misconduct and subject to sanctions including instant dismissal.

   Note: Although the seriousness of the situation must be emphasised, some leniency may be required where, say, a more junior employee, unwittingly disclosed price-sensitive information to someone not authorised to receive it.

4. The undertaking (senior employees)

   • All information originated, amended or processed in any way for or from the Board, or any committee of senior management, or connected with the preparation of the company's Annual and Interim Reports is to be regarded as totally confidential.

   • All backup information, graphics, data, statistics etc., prepared for or as a result of such work is similarly totally confidential.

   • No information can be divulged to any person below the level of senior management without the previous written authority of the [Chairman].

   • Nothing covered by items in this Undertaking may be removed from the [organisation] premises without the prior written authority of the [Chairman]. No other information may be removed from [organisation] premises without the prior written (and express) authority of a [Director].

• Infringements of this undertaking (which could in turn, and amongst other things) lead to the breaking of Stock Exchange rules and legislation, will be regarded as the most serious breach of company rules which could lead to dismissal.

• No information which in any way could be regarded as price-sensitive may be divulged to anyone other than signatories to this undertaking or to retained company advisors themselves working under a professional obligation to preserve confidentiality.

Note: It may be necessary to warn against persons claiming to be members of, say, the audit team, telephoning to 'discuss' the figures, hoping that the respondent will disclose information unwittingly. Where there is a possibility of such espionage, the use of alpha/numeric passwords may be necessary.

• Similar restrictions to the above apply to all [organisation] material, including (but not exclusively) product development work, research data, personnel information, etc., etc.

• All those required to sign such an undertaking must do so in the presence of a witness able to verify their identity.

5. The undertaking (junior employees)

    • The work of the [organisation] which consists of [detail], must at all times, be treated as confidential and protected from disclosure. It is an express condition of employment that no employee may divulge to a person outside the [organisation] any such information, or aid the outward transmission of any such information or data.

    • All backup information, graphics, data, statistics, reports, etc., prepared for or obtained as a result of such work and activity is similarly totally confidential to the [organisation] and must only be used for its purposes.

    • No such information may be removed from the [organisation] premises (other than in the ordinary course of business) without the prior written (and express) authority of a [Director].

    • Any deliberate infringement of these rules will be regarded as a most serious breach of organisation rules and could lead to instant dismissal. Accidental breach, due to negligence, will also be regarded as a breach of rules and may be subject to disciplinary action.

    • All those required to sign such an undertaking must do so in the presence of a witness able to verify their identity.

Other security aspects

It may be appropriate at this point to consider two further aspects of required behaviour although here it will tend to be the required behaviour of employees rather than Directors. The development and reliance on computer systems and intranets, whilst providing enhanced access to a mass of data, entails both security and relationship problems highlighted in the checklists overleaf and on page 178.

Computer system protection

The Computer Misuse Act 1990 makes offences of:

- Unauthorised access to computer material (i.e. both hacking and access by unauthorised users)

- Unauthorised change of computer material e.g. the insertion of a time bomb (e.g. the March 6th/ Michelangelo bug) and data destruction glitches (e.g. the Friday 13th bug), and

- Ulterior intent (i.e. unauthorised access for the purpose of committing a crime).

Penalties for unauthorised access (apart from those provided for under the Act which can be as much as five years imprisonment and/or an unlimited fine) can include dismissal for employees. Thus the Employment Appeal Tribunal (EAT) held in the *Denco v Joinson* case that an employee was fairly dismissed when he gained unauthorised access to his employer's computer system (including its payroll files) even though no purpose, other than curiosity, was the cause and no 'loss' (other than of the integrity of the system) occurred.

In that case the EAT commented that organisations should make it clear to their employees that unauthorised use of its computer system carries severe penalties – the following is suggested:

1. Employees may only operate within the areas of their own departmental operations and service areas. Access to other areas is restricted to authorised personnel only. Access to the systems of the organisation, particularly, but not exclusively, the computer systems, is reserved to authorised personnel only.

2. Unauthorised access to, or in any way tampering with, any computer system or software, or computer installation (including but not restricted to the items in this rule) will be regarded as gross misconduct and will render the offender liable to dismissal.

3. All computer records will be backed up daily (or more often if required) with back up stored in (a remote location). Data files altered during daily working will also be backed up daily with back up disks stored in (a remote location).

4. In no instance should any computer owned or leased by the business be used for playing games or any purpose other than the legitimate work of the business.

5. No software and/or discs etc. other than those owned or leased by the business must be used in the business computers.

6. All software and discs must be purchased new from recognised and reputable suppliers, backed by a confirmation that all such items are free from viruses etc., and/or with a guarantee/liability acceptance in the event that virus(es) which have caused damage, were present on purchase.

7. Anti-virus programs should be used regularly (specify intervals) to check that all systems, software and discs etc. (including back up files) are virus free. Any item found to be infected must be immediately separated from any networking arrangement, and steps taken to eliminate the virus.

Electronic mail

The use of computers linked via an intranet to allow the instant transmission of messages via internal 'e-mail' enables non-typists to generate messages. In turn this has led in many cases to an 'over casual' approach to the generation of such messages.

In addition the ability to generate instant responses (particularly when angry) rather than needing to wait for a letter to be typed has led to instances where ill-considered, overhasty and even rude replies have been generated – and later regretted. To avoid its use for abuse and harassment etc., (as well as the creation of unwanted and unintended contracts) the Board may wish to consider introducing some controls over the use (and particularly the abuse) of the system.

Electronic transmissions policy

1. E-mail should be used primarily to distribute/update information, confirm arrangements, confirm meetings etc.

2. As an exception the system can be used to leave messages where the recipient is unavailable and the message awaits their return.

3. E-mails should not be used as a substitute for face to face or telephone conversation.

    (Note: This substitution for personal interfacing and two-way communication is one of the most worrying aspects of the use of e-mail).

4. E-mail information cannot substitute for managerial control and should not be attempted to be used as such.

5. On no account should the system be used for vindictive, harassing, discriminatory or abusive comment or criticism of anyone, whether this is the target, another employee or any third party.

6. All opinions expressed on another should only be based on and backed up by facts.

7. Items for dissemination via e-mail should be checked after drafting to ensure clarity and accuracy of message.

8. A person in receipt of an item which they feel should have been prohibited by 3 above should notify [name].

9. Any person proved to have deliberately sent an item prohibited by item three above will be deemed guilty of gross misconduct and will be dealt with under the disciplinary procedure accordingly.

10. All messages etc., should be clear and unambiguous and coded from 5 star to 0 star in order of priority. Clarity is preferable to brevity. Jargon should be avoided in the interests of clarity.

11. An e-mail message should be treated as if it were a hard copy letter and drafted and checked in the same way.

12. No response to an e-mail message should ever be sent in haste, anger or hostility. Ideally several hours should elapse between drafting and sending a reply (following reconsideration).

Notes:

1. When using electronic transmission for sending letters, orders, invoices etc. to third parties, companies should ensure that the document complies with the requirements of the Companies Act and bears the company's registered name, office and number and the country of registration.

2. Although it can be difficult to imply a binding contract from a telephone call, if e-mail is used in the same way as a telephone call, a binding contract could be inferred – there is after all permanent evidence of the message. It may be advisable to require all external correspondence to carry a disclaimer to attempt to indemnify the sponsoring company against improper use of electronic messages or to stipulate that a contractual relationship will only exist when confirmed in hardcopy.

Insider dealing rules

Included on page 172 (draft confidentiality policy) and related only to companies whose shares are listed on a Stock Exchange are concerns over a lack of discretion or deliberate leaking of information in a Director's possession which could be price-sensitive. The principle of the Stock Exchange is that all who deal in shares should have the same information available to them. Hence all information the company wishes to disclose must be made public simultaneously (most often by means of the publication of its Preliminary Announcement which gives a résumé of the results for the latest financial year – see Chapter 13). Inevitably Directors (and other senior managers) will be privy to information at this and other times which if published might affect the share price. Such data is known as price sensitive information and it is inherent in the position of Director that it should not be disclosed other than where running the business so demands. If such data is disclosed other than at the required time and to the required people who then trade in the shares, that act and the act of providing the information is known as Insider Dealing.

The Criminal Justice Act 1993 lists three instances where insider dealing occurs:

1. If an individual who has inside information deals in securities using such inside information. Thus if you are the Director of a public company and knowing that information to which you were a party would affect the price of the shares were it to be made public, and you then traded in the shares, you could be held to be guilty of insider dealing.

2. If an individual who has inside information encourages another person to trade in the shares he may be guilty of insider dealing and if the person who is encouraged to deal knows that the data is 'inside information' because the informant is in a position to have access to such information then that person may also be guilty.

3. If a person discloses price sensitive information to another person other than in the proper performance of his duties. Thus, if a Director told his wife who then traded in the shares on the basis of the information then she would be guilty. If the Director's wife told a friend and that friend knows the Director's position in the company and thus that the source of the information is likely to be authoritative, then if they trade in the shares, they may also be guilty. Thus a person in no way connected to the company (other than by knowing the data) can nevertheless be guilty.

Similarly, if a Director has a professional adviser – e.g. an accountant – looking after his interests and they learn the information and trade then they too will be guilty.

For those found guilty – the penalties are severe – up to seven years imprisonment and/or a fine.

There are some defences including 'that the act of trading would have taken place whether the inside information had been known or not'. This should cover the situation where the person concerned needs to sell shares in order to raise money for a specific (and presumably time-related) purpose. In addition if a Director disclosed the information in the ordinary course of business not believing it would be used for the purposes covered by the Act then that should also be a good defence. There have been around 30 cases brought under the Insider Dealing Regulations and at least two jail sentences imposed.

WARNING: Despite the legislation it is recognised that much insider dealing does take place although it is difficult to bring charges. Currently the government is considering granting to regulatory bodies power to take civil action where criminal action is unlikely to succeed.

Share trading

The custom of requiring Directors to hold shares in companies to whose Board they were appointed has tended to die out. However, recently, not least due to the suggestion made in the Cadbury report that this was advisable, there seems to have been a growing pressure to encourage Directors of PLCs to hold shares in their companies. This poses them a problem in terms of the timing of any purchases and/or sales since almost inevitably at every stage in their company's financial calendar they will have access to information which, if released, could have an effect on the share price. In recognition of this the Stock Exchange listing agreement suggests that Directors should observe a two-month 'dead period' before the publication of interim or preliminary announcements during which time Directors should not buy or sell any of their companies shares other than for the most urgent reasons. In addition, most companies now require their Directors to notify the Chairman every time they trade in shares or options. Some companies apply wider time limits than those suggested.

Summary
checklist

✓ Generate, promulgate and police a code of
ethics/behaviour.

✓ Generate, promulgate and police a
confidentiality undertaking (possibly
devising two or more versions depending
on seniority of signatories).

✓ Generate, promulgate and police computer
and e-mail undertakings.

✓ Brief all Directors and officers re insider
dealing restrictions and any 'dead' periods
for trading on an ongoing basis.

chapter ten

'He who communicates leads'

Leadership and management

Distinguishing between leadership and management

Definition

The chapter title is derived from a saying of Jack Jones, the former General Secretary of the Transport and General Workers Union. Another quotation, this time from Steven Covey, the American business author and leadership guru, may highlight the differences between these two types of control. Covey suggests that 'management is all about doing things right, but leadership is all about doing the right things'. Circumscribed as it is by legislation there is a great danger in considering the work of the effective Director that we concentrate so much on 'doing things right' that we overlook the overriding need for the company – and particularly the Directors leading the company – to do the right things. In this context, doing the right things involves planning and managing the company – or in the widest sense of the word, providing leadership to all who work for it. Thus, as well as complying with all their legal obligations Directors must take the initiative in terms of 'leading' their companies and above all their employees. The concept of leadership should be obvious and yet experience suggests that perhaps because it is deemed to be so obvious it is taken for granted and thus is ignored in too many organisations. In too many instances Boards of Directors have become aloof and disconnected from the team they have a duty to lead. Such a situation can only operate to the detriment of the organisation and its customers – and thus render its performance far less effective than possible.

There are innumerable books about leadership and there is no doubt that good leadership can be improved by the guidance thus provided. Whilst this may be so it does seem that the best leaders tend to operate more by instinct for what is their view of the 'best' solution rather than as a result of learning what is a 'good practice'. Perhaps their guidance in making the 'right' decision and taking the 'right' approach is derived from the 'do-as-you-would-be-done-by' dictum – i.e. 'if it were me that was affected by this decision, rather than me making it, how would I react?' Appreciating how the other party to a decision will react is critical to good management or leadership. This does not mean that the decision should be altered but that if we appreciate likely reactions before acting we may be guided to modify our approach, which if we then receive a more positive reaction can mean we gain where a poorer, less perceptive approach may have generated a negative reaction.

Leadership qualities

In carrying out around 100 lectures throughout the UK over the past five years, I probed the question of leadership and what those being led wished to receive from their managers. The five most valued (and wanted) characteristics that the considerable majority of those questioned (approximately 2,000 supervisors) wished to obtain from their managers can be summarised and grouped into a useful mnemonic shown below:

A manager's most wanted qualities

The ability and preparedness to:

- Listen

- Encourage

- Advise

- Delegate

- Support

In other words in being a good manager, the person LEADS.

Listen

Sir John Harvey-Jones suggests that 'the ability to listen is the rarest of all characteristics. Listening is all about what people don't say.' Perhaps it is unsurprising that real active listening is such a rare commodity considering that at school (and indeed before our formal schooling starts) we may be taught to talk, taught to look, taught to read but rarely these days taught to listen. Children are taught to express themselves without necessarily being encouraged to listen to others expressing themselves – the result leans towards a figurative Tower of Babel!

Similarly in later life Directors are subjected to a vast amount of data coming at them from all directions. In such a situation it can be very difficult to find time to listen to one's subordinates but it is only if such time is found (which may be where the fourth characteristic in the above figure is all-important) that mutual respect can be fostered and the Director will gain an insight into the true attitude and feelings of the subordinate. Too many Directors claim to 'know what my people are thinking' – which, even if they practice active listening, is likely to be nothing more nor less than a dangerous self-delusion and displays both a conceit and a breathtaking arrogance. Actively listening to members of one's team and observing their actions may give a more accurate guide to the way they are feeling.

Active listening takes time – time which preferably should not be interrupted by phones ringing, visitors or unwanted distractions. If any of the latter are present and are allowed to interrupt, then the message being conveyed to the other party is 'you are not as important as this item which has interrupted us' which is hardly guaranteed to impress, motivate or incentivise the other party.

Requirements for active listening

a)   Allow sufficient time for the interface

b)   Allow the other party to talk without interrupting

c)   Take the phone off the hook and close the door to visitors

d) Pay attention to what is being said (and not said)

e) Show that you are concentrating on what is being said

f) Ask questions (even if not essential to your understanding) to demonstrate that you are concentrating and understand the theme

g) Watch the other party's body language to try to gauge whether or not they are being accurate and truthful

h) Watch your own body language to ensure you are giving signals which indicate you are paying attention

i) Don't make snap decisions – ask for time to consider points or requests made

j) Make notes but don't doodle

k) Don't interrupt except to ask for more clarification of a point made

l) Don't dismiss points out of hand – if you don't agree prepare arguments which counter the points made

and so on.

Notes:

1. The essential ingredient is time. Even if the answer is no, if sufficient time has been allowed to the other party to put their viewpoint, they may feel that justice has been done.

2. The antithesis of this positive approach is never to listen but merely to make decisions from the manager's sole viewpoint. Sometimes the right decision will be made and respect may be gained – often it will not and respect will be nil. It is virtually impossible to lead those who have no respect.

Encourage

Few are able or chosen to be leaders. Most people are content to be led – to follow the lead and participate as members of a team (remembering the adages 'Together Everyone Achieves More' and 'None of us is as good as all of us'). Most are also prepared to put up with strict regimes – provided they are fair. In a recent survey 87 per cent of those asked stated that what they most wanted from employment was to be treated fairly, whilst over 70 per cent stated they needed to be encouraged and stimulated in their work. It is reckoned that a sizable proportion of people are capable of performing well at one level above that at which they currently perform. An effective manager will recognise this and by encouragement attempt to show team members how to take on more responsibility and to develop.

(Note: The antithesis here is to insist people do as they are told and not encourage them to make suggestions, ask for help etc. In such a situation it is hardly surprising if mistakes are made or there is no commitment to working together.)

Advise

In most instances a manager should have a reasonable command of the rudiments of all the tasks being undertaken by his team, if not the actual detail. With this knowledge they should be able to provide advice if one of those team members requires assistance in carrying out their duties.

(Note: Failing to provide advice (which entails a failure to listen actively) will demotivate the team member – who else can they turn to if not to their manager?)

Delegate

Faced with the need to listen, to encourage and to advise and provide support to their team members many managers will retreat behind the age-old complaints (or excuses) 'insufficient time' or 'too busy on my own work'. It should be pointed out to such 'managers' that the main task of a manager is to 'manage' i.e. to direct and lead those who report to them and this is their priority. The job of a manager is not to do the job themselves, even if they are able to carry out the duties more accurately and swiftly than their subordinates, but to ensure that the latter carry out the duties providing assistance when necessary. Many of the more routine duties undertaken by managers could, with a little training and guidance be carried out by more junior employees which has the advantage of:

- Freeing the manager's time

- Making the subordinate's job more interesting

- Encouraging commitment from the team members by demonstrating management's faith and confidence in them.

Principles of effective delegation

a) Assess (on an ongoing basis) the subordinate for capability and willingness to assume a greater workload

b) Establish precisely the duties, responsibilities AND authority that are to be delegated

c) Check whether the subordinate can assume extra duties delineated immediately or needs training, or a delay before taking over such duties (and check regularly after delegation)

d) Delegate only to those able to carry out the work

e) Brief and train the delegatee to carry out the work

f)   Advise all involved of the delegation

g)   Provide time, support and guidance for the delegatee (ongoing)

h)   Avoid the destruction of confidence by undercutting the authority of delegatee

i)   Regularly review progress and accomplishments

j)   Constantly support and motivate – never denigrate.

Support

If the manager is really leading and his subordinates are team members, there will be mutual support – although the team may only be as good as its leader, the leader will only be as good as his team. However, by providing support and encouragement at the required times, good leaders can make members of a team perform above themselves. In truth the total performance can be greater than the sum of the parts – and in reality 'together everyone achieves more'. Many people lack self-confidence, but with the support of their manager or leader, often they can achieve at a level that they never thought possible.

Maximising human resource

If Directors are responsible for maximising the value of the assets of their company and those that work for the company are the greatest assets of their company, then there is no more important task for the Directors than obtaining the greatest output from the company's human assets. Whilst this can be done via positive leadership, it is unlikely to be achieved by issuing dictats from a position remote from such assets – yet this is how many Directors try to direct their employees. We could perhaps summarise this human asset management in the checklist opposite.

Guidelines of good leadership/management

a) Build a team and constantly work with it and as part of it to make it achieve its aims

b) Clearly define and set the task for the team (use unambiguous and clear language) and coach and support those required to achieve it

c) Manage (i.e. lead by listening, encouraging, advising and supporting) the team members

d) Talk to and actively listen to each member of the team – creating mutual respect

e) Delegate (or empower) to as great an extent as possible so that you can stand back, plan for the future and manage the team members

f) Discuss problems and use suggestions and ideas from those involved

g) Use organisation charts to demonstrate relationships without letting them become straitjackets

h) Outlaw demarcation disputes – resolve altercations via discussions

i) Draw solutions from those at the sharp end rather than imposing solutions on them

j) Be visible, approachable, and patient.

(Note: These guidelines are applicable to the teams led by Directors. However, each Director needs to ensure that each management level in turn leads their teams in the same way.)

Additional guidelines

- Acknowledge achievement – praise is an extremely effective means of motivation (and it is free!) – but to be really effective it must be genuine

- Monitor and demonstrate progress – if we praise progress, then when there is no progress, the need for effort and objective criticism is obvious

- Share the preferred tasks – and the awkward tasks, so that all members of the team take their turn at both – example is a powerful motivator

- Encourage team members to discuss their concerns and problems – to think positively thereby helping create a better team spirit.

Management is a continuing responsibility – everything about the role is ongoing – and no-one should be more aware of this than the Board of the Directors whose view must always be partly focussed on the long-term. Whilst setting up the principles and practice of good management/ leadership is essential – so too is a commitment to continuing this approach which may be a harder task than actually starting. When things are up and running, we need to continue to stimulate attention; good leaders understand the need for consistency of approach. The items set out in the checklist below may provide a reminder of what is required.

Ongoing requirements of leadership

1. Give praise when merited

In the UK we tend to criticise too often and praise too little. Yet praise is incredibly cost-effective and usually very motivational. Most people want recognition and respond positively to it. If we give praise when things are done well then we will find it easier to achieve a positive response when we have to criticise.

2.   Provide incentives and rewards

Simple praise may be a valuable motivational force but it needs to be substantiated by material recognition – money, vouchers, etc. which reflect the genuine appreciation of the organisation for good work etc. Peer recognition can be a valuable aid in motivation.

3.   Training

Being prepared to invest in employees by means of funding (or even part funding) training for the mutual benefit of employee and employer can not only motivate employees but also retain the best performers. Research indicates that in some fast moving industries good calibre people tend to be attracted to employers who will provide career training and/or that the provision of training can aid the retention of better calibre staff.

4.   Counselling

From time to time most employees will encounter problems that can affect their performance. Encouraging them to use a confidential counselling service can not only assist solutions but also demonstrate the wish of the organisation to provide assistance. Stress is a major cause of poor performance and absenteeism. An employee under stress cannot perform to the best of their ability. Genuinely assisting or being prepared to assist the employee under stress (whether work or home-generated) should help relieve the stress and return full productivity. The benefits on the rest of the team should not be underestimated.

5.   Flexibility of relationship

Flexibility of working, of attitudes, of rules, and so on, create an ambience of a partnership between organisation and employee. Nowadays there is increasingly a recognition that there is a need to provide a balance between the demands of employees' own lives and their working lives. The relationship is moving to one between equal partners where 'give and take' is required from both, rather the blind obedience of the 'master and servant' relationship of the recent past.

6. Flexibility of work

If there is a variety of relatively straightforward (even boring jobs) try to train personnel so that they can periodically have a change round. In this way, new relationships as well as new approaches may result. Indeed, it may be that someone newly performing a task will see a way in which it could be improved.

7. Listening

Team briefing, quality circles, workplace forums, improvement groups, suggestion schemes may all play a part in encouraging thought about the jobs and the way they are performed – and in welding a team together. Often it is the simple fact of leader and team talking and discussing matters which is the conduit through which the results are achieved.

8. Delegate and empower

Responsibility should be pushed as far down as possible. This will leave time for man/woman management as well as making the delegatee's job more rewarding. Encouraging employees themselves to work in teams harnesses peer pressure, which should then tend to improve output and communication and generate a willingness to take on more responsibility and tasks.

....

Communication principles

The key to the whole question of management or leadership is communication – a concept which is not fully understood despite the millions of words written on the subject. Leading consultants McKinsey estimate that by the year 2000, 70 per cent of all European jobs will require professional skills (that is 'A' levels or higher). The Confederation of British Industry, commenting on this research stated that 'outstanding communication skills' will be needed by these employees.

The problem is that the word 'communication' is often misused and those guilty of such misuse are often those at Director level and include:

- Those who claim 'our communication is excellent' and in evidence produce handbooks, Annual Reports, procedure manuals, newsletters and so on. Such documentation may be excellent – and essential – but it is not communication

- Those who state that their internal communication is first class because their chief executive regularly makes presentations to the employees. This is admirable and valuable but it is not communication

- Those who describe the provision of excellent product and service data to their customers as 'first class communication'. Again the documentation is of real value – but it is not communication.

Information is NOT communication

That 'we have a communication problem' may be true – but in reality 'we' have three problems – of definition, of application and of interpretation.

a) Definition. The definition problem is, simply stated, absolutely vital but often entirely overlooked. We tend to use the word 'communication' when actually we mean 'information'.

If A, a manager, tells B (a member of his staff) that there is a requirement for B to produce 1000 widgets by next Friday (or, worse, sends him an e-mail or memo), very often A will regard himself as having communicated with B. In fact all that has happened is that B is in receipt of an instruction or some information (which he may or may not understand). If B is in the situation that he has half his team away sick, there is an overtime ban preventing the remaining part of the team from working longer and there is a problem obtaining raw material from stores, there is little possibility of him complying with A's request. However, only if B replies 'no chance' and explains his problems (i.e. provides feedback) does a communicative process start.

b) Application. As its name implies 'co-mmunication' requires a dialogue – a meeting of minds between two or more parties. Where the parties are face to face it is possible that communication will ensue even if it was not intended. If the two are face to face, B's body language, even if he utters no words, may well provide a message to A (provided A is prepared to look for and appreciate such messages). It is said that, when face to face, words are only 7 per cent of the message – body language, tone, situation etc. provide 93 per cent.

However, face to face communication, invaluable although it is, is possible in only a minority of the instances when we wish to 'communicate' with our target audience. Or do we wish to communicate at all? Are we not in the position that all we want to do is to inform them? There is nothing wrong with informing – indeed it may be essential and, in some cases, even a legal requirement. The danger comes when we assume that this one way simple (easy to generate) provision of information is the same as a dynamic, two-way dialogue which is the only true communication.

c) Interpretation. Because we learned to talk without formal teaching and others tend to reply when we use the skill, we assume that we know how to communicate and that others will always understand what we mean. However, research indicates that such an assumption is false.

Communication barriers

- If we read information (without making notes) on average our memories will retain around 10 per cent of the subject matter

- If we hear information (with no opportunity to ask questions or take notes) we will retain around 20 per cent

- If we see information (e.g. a video) we will retain about 30 per cent

- If we see and hear information (for example at a presentation) we will retain about 50 per cent

- If we are involved in the information provision so that we have an input we will retain about 70 per cent

- If the information is provided in a learning situation (e.g. a trainee talks his/her way through a process) we will retain about 90 per cent.

The golden rule to remember in seeking to start communicating is to frame the data with the interests of the target audience in mind. (As a corollary it may be worth recording that, when providing written information, if the reader doesn't understand it – it is the writer's responsibility.)

Nowadays in addition to traditional means of conveying information there is a whole panoply of technological developments – faxes, voice-mail, e-mail, the internet, intranets and so on. In truth we have a magnificent range of excellent information transmission tools. Such developments are obviously welcome but we need to guard against assuming that in using them we are communicating (or, even worse, are improving communication) – we are not – all we have done is speed up the transmission and recording of information – nothing more. The barriers to communication set out above remain.

Putting the requirement in perspective

The following quotations may place the challenge in perspective:

- Management guru Peter Drucker said recently 'The solutions to organisational problems frequently lie not in the executive suite but in the collective intelligence of the workforce'

- The report *Impact of People Management Practices on Business Performance* concludes '...if managers wish to influence the performance of their companies the most important area they should emphasise is the management of people. This is ironic, given that our research has also demonstrated that emphasis on human resource management is one of the most neglected areas of managerial practice within organisations'

- In reviewing worldwide communication research over the last 20 years, Dr Jon White of the City University Business School found a consistent correlation between high business performance and good organisational communication

- Franklin D Roosevelt said 'The art of being a great leader is to get people to do what you want them to do because they want to do it.' If we seek to lead we need first to communicate. Those who communicate will lead – if it is not the Directors who communicate then whoever is will be 'doing the leading'.

Briefings

Inevitably time constraints will mean that even if we wish to interface individually this is impossible other than on isolated occasions (e.g. when conducting appraisal or performance review interviews which is one occasion when active listening is essential – and interruptions should be outlawed). Accordingly we may need to use other means to communicate, for example, briefing either of the team interfacing with their immediate leader or by Directors interfacing with groups of employees. For many years the Industrial Society (particularly when led by John Garnett who was both an inspirational speaker and leader) espoused the concept of 'cascade briefing' whereby Directors brief senior managers who brief middle managers who brief junior managers who brief supervisors who brief those at the sharp end – the information thus cascades down the chain of command. Whilst this process is better than nothing, it has limitations. Each time a message is repeated it tends to lose 10-15 per cent of the content – or worse a different 10-15 per cent is substituted and thus a kind of 'Chinese whisper' game develops. In addition some of those required to brief in turn will be less adept at it than others – and thus less willing to do it. Others may not wish to pass on messages but to hoard them to preserve their power base.

To some extent these problems can be overcome by Directors issuing a back up brief so that the essentials are provided in writing. However, the most glaring deficiency is that the process is not communication at all since the data is flowing only one way. Unless the process is also reversed so that queries flow up the chain of command (in which case they may be more likely to be filtered out by intervening levels of management) the required two-way aspect of communication does not exist at all. This can be overcome if one Director carries out all the briefings. This has a triple advantage:

- The messages to all are likely to be the same

- Authoritative answers are likely to be given to employees asking for additional information/ clarification and

- The true unfiltered views of the workforce will be fed directly to the Board.

Best practice audit

Boards cannot afford to assume that the practices they wish their managers to adopt are being implemented and a regular check on how well the company is being led may be advisable. The questions set out in the checklist below may provide a base. Ideally each answer should be 'yes'!

How are we managing?

1. Have we devised plans and discussed their implementation with employees so that the employees themselves 'own' the plans to gain their active commitment to them?

2. Do we encourage employees to make suggestions and constructive criticism about the company, its products, procedures and endeavours?

3. Is there mutual respect between management and employees and are the pressures on employees in terms of working and private lives balanced?

4. Does management listen actively to employees and vice versa on every occasion so that the full facts and implications of all matters are exposed?

5. Are initiatives introduced via consultation and agreement thereby generating a 'yes' reaction and a genuine commitment (rather than by dictat which can often generate a 'no' reaction)?

6. Does everyone involved realise that as part of a single team their objective is to satisfy their customer in order to achieve the aims of the organisation?

7. Is training provided and are employees encouraged to develop their skills and talents at all times?

8. Do managers and employees work in job-related teams mutually helping solve problems, to attain (or exceed) output targets that they have agreed?

9. Is there an open culture whereby information flows both ways thus generating genuine two way communication – and is this situation confirmed by the employees?

10. Are employees proud to state that they work for the organisation?

Summary checklist

✓ Directors need to provide leadership to ensure all those involved work towards the aims set for the company.

✓ Managers need to adopt leadership techniques – active listening, encouragement, advice provision, delegation and support to those they lead.

✓ Directors need to ensure that quality communication exists within their companies remembering that information is not the same as communication.

✓ People respond to the provision of information and the opportunity to communicate and have a wealth of ideas which can be used for the positive benefit of the company – who knows how to do the job, and how to improve it better than the person doing it?

✓ Direct 'Board to sharp end' interfacing should provide the best communication interface.

✓ Regular audits of personnel practice and interfacing should be conducted.

chapter eleven

Meeting the owners

Shareholders' meetings

The Annual General Meeting

'The AGM is often the only opportunity for the small shareholder to be fully briefed on the company's activities and to question senior managers on both operation and governance matters' – report of the Hampel Committee.

Since they are appointed by the shareholders, Directors are required by Company Law to report regularly to the shareholders and to give an account of their stewardship of the assets entrusted to them. Within 18 months of incorporation and thereafter at not more than 15 month intervals, a company must hold an Annual General Meeting (AGM). Unfortunately because the holding of the meeting and the business which must be transacted at such a meeting are both prescribed by law, most AGMs tend to be very formal, even legalistic, events at which there is often very little meaningful account given of the Directors' stewardship.

Although it is true that financial results are provided via the Annual Report (in which very often the notice convening the AGM is contained) as we shall see in Chapter 12 the information given in many reports is couched in a format that most non-financially aware shareholders find unhelpful and uninformative. Unfortunately in some cases this is not only effect but also cause since such Boards really pay only lip service to the concept of their accountability to the shareholders and seem to minimise the amount and clarity of information they provide.

As there is increased interest in the activities of wealth-creating companies and in their power and control changes, may be forced on those adopting such attitudes. Indeed in the final report of the Hampel Committee on Corporate Governance it is suggested that at AGMs 'which are well attended' the Board should make a business presentation which could force greater disclosure of plans and aspirations. The words 'which are well attended' are apposite. One can imagine that if few shareholders attend (other than Board members and their families) there would be little point in the Board spending considerable time preparing such a presentation but on the other the fact that so few attend is probably a result of the general belief that shareholders learn next to nothing at the AGM. Of course an awareness that a business presentation was to be made might actually encourage greater attendance and thus greater interest – in turn creating greater demand for increased transparency of activities and results, and for improved accountability.

The Hampel Report also suggests that where a shareholder raises a matter at the AGM which cannot be answered at the time, the Chairman should provide a written answer subsequently and the Board should be prepared to enter into a 'dialogue based on a mutual understanding of objectives.' This echoes the moves being made by several leading institutional share investors to take a more active role by exercising their voting rights at General Meetings.

In 1996 the DTI issued a consultative document seeking views regarding increasing the rights of shareholders to ask questions at General Meetings whilst Margaret Beckett, launching of Government's review of Company Law ('Modern Company Law for a Competitive Economy') referred to 'transparent stewardship' (of institutional investors exercising voting rights on behalf of their investors) requiring 'positive use of voting rights'. Generally AGMs of the future may be more informative and meaningful than many have been in the past. Whilst much of the thrust of the foregoing applies to listed PLCs rather to private LTDs, it may be the precursor of a general move towards greater accountability of all Boards to their shareholders.

Notice

The prescribed notice must be given of the AGM. The meeting needs 21 days clear notice, with 'clear' meaning that neither the day the notice is posted nor the day of the meeting count towards the 21. In addition, care should be taken as notices posted by 1st class post are deemed to take two days to arrive whilst notice cannot be served on a non-business day. Thus a notice posted on (say) Thursday 21st May would not arrive until Saturday 23rd May but could not be deemed to be served until Tuesday 26th May (25th May being a Bank Holiday). 26th May would then count as day one of the 21 day period. Thus the earliest the meeting could be convened would be Tuesday 16th June (i.e. 27 days after posting).

Notes:

a) Only 20 clear days notice is required for companies registered in Scotland.

b) If all the members entitled to be present so vote the requirement for notice can be dispensed with.

c) The Hampel Committee endorsed the suggestion made by the Chartered Institute of Secretaries that meetings should be convened giving at least 20 WORKING days notice. (In the example given above of the notice being sent on 16th May this, if adopted, would mean the meeting could not be held until 23rd June – as all Bank Holidays and weekends must be excluded.)

Whilst the AGM of a 'Director-owned' or 'family-owned' company may be little more than a formality, that of any company where there are shareholders outside the Board (and particularly if the company is Stock Exchange listed) is an occasion when the corporate entity is 'on display'. For that reason, the meeting needs careful planning to ensure that the company is seen in the best possible 'light'. Whether the meeting is to be such a promotional showcase, or is regarded more as an administrative chore, it still needs adequate preparation, and at least the items set out in the checklist opposite need attention. The checklist included in Chapter 12 for the production of the Annual Report needs to be considered in conjunction with this checklist.

AGM preparation

1. Prepare list/timetable of all items needing to be addressed

2. Allocate items to named delegatees – as in following example:

Item	Responsibility
Decide date and time	Board
Visit venue, check facilities	Co.Sec/Board
Book venue (6/12 months ahead)	Co.Sec/Board

Check:

- Room and overflow facility

- Air conditioning/ventilation

- Acoustics/amplification

- Accommodation including catering/toilet facilities

- Notice Boards/room directions

- Tables for signing in.

If product/services display required:

- Display tables/pin or felt Boards

- Computer graphics, etc.

Stipulate – timetable for arrivals:

- Serving tea/coffee

- Lunch (if required)

- Likely departure

[Those responsible will need to indicate responsibility for all items following]

Delegate items to staff e.g:

- Greeting arrivals

- Ensuring arrivals sign in

- Ushering to seats

- Care of Registers and Proxies

- Act as teller (in event of poll)

- Care of statutory and minute books, service contracts, etc.

- Liaison with catering

- Checking arrival of proposers/seconders (and arranging substitutions in event of absence)

- Display of products/tour of premises

- Preparation of Chairman's crib (i.e. a script to cover each part of the meeting – see below)

- Preparation of and answers to awkward questions

- Preparation of Board presentation

- Briefing on preparations, likely problems etc. (i.e. a meeting scenario) for Board and advisers

- Liaison with auditors, solicitors, brokers, public relations (and, through them, media representatives)

- Liaison with company registrar (including printing of tax vouchers/dividend warrants and arrangements for giving authority to post)

- Transport arrangements (particularly for guests).

3. Ensure all delegatees understand requirements

   Newcomers to the task should be fully briefed in the requirements and their progress checked regularly. Those who have not attended an AGM previously should be required to attend the AGMs of a few listed PLCs to gain an insight into procedure.

4 Recheck preparations one month prior to event

   The attention to detail is essential to ensure the public showing of the company is smooth and efficient. It will, after all be a reflection of how the company operates.

5. Consider style/content to be adopted with Chairman/ Board.

Some companies are making their AGM less formal – even advertising that members of the Board will be available before or after the meeting for individual discussion. If the company adopts the Hampel recommendation of making a business presentation this could help comprehension of strategy (and even aid Board support in the event of a hostile takeover bid).

6. Coach spokespersons in handling the media particularly in dealing with hostile or critical questioning. Unless well-prepared and well-briefed for this type of examination, reputations (of both person and company) can be irreparably damaged and unnecessarily bad impressions provided.

7. Obtain advice on difficult questions which might be asked. Not only is it important to contact supportive shareholders to obtain proxy if not attending, and to arrange tame 'proposers' and 'seconders' to avoid silences at the meeting when the Chairman invites nominations etc., it is also essential that if hostility is expected, then it is prepared for, as follows:

   • Identify source and extent of support and of opposition

   • Ensure 'hostiles' have a right of attendance

   • If time allows, consider possibility of a private meeting to avoid public confrontation

   • Monitor arrivals – arrange for security forces to be nearby to deal with any physical disruption

   • Canvass proxies sufficient to ensure overcoming any potential opposition

   • Prepare a list of the questions least wished to be asked – and a crib of suitable answers

   • Brief the Directors concerned of the source of the problem and the steps taken to control/deal with it

- Brief media contacts and provide media trained spokesman to answer follow up queries

- If hostile shareholders wish to make a point they should be allowed such a courtesy, answering the points made as far as possible and offering subsequent discussions if this is feasible.

8. Prepare required documentation including:

   a) Letter of invitation

   b) Arrangements for Directors

   c) Attendance card

   d) Admission cards

   e) Proxy

   f) Mailing list application

   g) Change of address form

   h) Dividend mandate form

   i) Product discount details (if applicable)

   j) Dividend/share exchange data (if applicable)

   k) Annual Report (see Chapter 12).

9. Prepare draft press release to follow conclusion of meeting. Whereas this may be able to be produced in advance where it is known that certain statements will be made, should hostility be anticipated the production of any press statement may need to be left until after the meeting. If hostility has been experienced some statement rather than 'no comment' is advisable.

Briefing the Chairman

Running a General Meeting is not the same as running a Board Meeting – particularly if the media and other outsiders are present. Those unfamiliar with or new to the process may find a brief or script of value. Rather than waiting for the meeting itself before using such a brief, it may be better to 'trial' it by suggesting the Chairman runs a dummy meeting using the script so that the Chairman is fully familiar with the process. The brief may then be used more as an aide-mémoire than script.

Script example

Chairman's crib for xxth Annual General Meeting to be held on (date)

ACTION (A): At (time) call meeting to order

SCRIPT (S): 'Ladies and Gentlemen I welcome you to the …th AGM of [Company name] Ltd/plc. We will now deal with the formal proceedings, following which you will be able to meet members of the Board and other executives and chat informally over some refreshments. We have, as you can see around you, provided displays of our products and services.

The Notice of this meeting was dispatched to all members of the Company on (date) and I will ask the Secretary to read the notice.'

  A: Secretary reads notice

  S: 'The first item on the agenda concerns the consideration of the Directors report with the report and accounts for the (twelve) months ended (date). Those accounts and the Balance Sheet as at that date have been audited by your auditor Messrs (Name) and I request Mr (name) a partner of that firm of registered auditors to deliver the Audit report.'

  A: Auditor reads report

  S: 'May I propose that the Report of the Directors, together with the annexed statement of the

Company's accounts for the (twelve) months ended and the Balance Sheet as at that date duly audited be now received, and adopted.'

(Note: Legally there is no need for these items to be adopted by the shareholders but as many assume it is, it may be easier to take this route and only if there is opposition to make the point that approval is not required.)

S: 'Has anyone any questions or comment?'

A: Pause – if questions are raised it will be necessary to deal with them or if they are of a technical/financial nature pass them to the Finance Director to answer.

S: 'As part of that proposal may I also propose that a final dividend of (amount) per cent or (amount) pence per share on the ordinary shares of the Company payable on (date) be now declared for the (twelve) months ended (date). I call upon (name) to second that proposal.'

A: Seconder speaks

S: 'All those in favour please raise your hands (pause). Anyone against (pause)'

A: Assess and declare result

Note: The Directors can pay an interim dividend without shareholder approval but need shareholder approval for a final dividend. The shareholders can either approve or reduce the final dividend – they cannot increase it. If the Board wish to ensure that the amount of the final dividend is paid (but suspect the shareholders might not approve it) it might be preferable to pay a second interim dividend – which does not need shareholder approval – and not to pay a final dividend at all.

S: 'I therefore declare the motion carried.'

S: 'Item 2 concerns the re-election of the retiring Director(s). The Director(s) retiring by rotation is/are and I have much pleasure in proposing that (name) be and he hereby is re-elected a Director of the Company. I will ask (name) to second that proposal.

A: Seconder speaks

S: 'All those in favour (pause) and against (pause). (Declare result)

I declare Mr (name) duly re-elected a Director of the company.'

Note: If more than one Director retires by rotation separate proposals are required for each unless an additional proposal to deal with all such re-elections as a single entity has first been passed. There may also be proposals needed to re-elect Directors who have been appointed since the previous AGM. Re-elected Directors may wish to express their thanks to the meeting.

S: 'Item 3 concerns the re-election of Messrs (auditors) as Auditors of the company and I call upon Mr (name) to propose that resolution and Mr (name) to second it'

A: Proposer and seconder speak

S: 'All those in favour (pause). Anyone against (pause). (Declare result)'

S: 'Item 4 authorises the Directors to fix the remuneration of the auditors and I will ask Mr (name) to propose that resolution and Mr (name) to second it'

A: Proposer and seconder speak

S: 'All those in favour (pause). Anyone against (pause). (Declare result)'

S: 'Is there any other ordinary business for consideration?'

(In fact other than the proposal of a vote of thanks to the Chairman/Board it is unlikely that anything else can be discussed by the meeting since notice of such business will not have been given although of course if all shareholders are present notice could be waived.)

S: 'I therefore declare this xxth AGM closed. Thank you.'

Making the record

Minutes

The following draft demonstrates how the Minutes of a meeting such as the one for which the above Chairman's brief was prepared might appear. Such Minutes should be prepared immediately after the conclusion of the meeting and approved as a true record by the Board at its next following Board Meeting. There is no need to send the Minutes to the shareholders or to have them available at the next following general meeting although shareholders have a right of inspection of the Minutes of their meetings and the Minutes must be held at the Registered Office for this purpose.

ANY OTHER COMPANY LTD 431(1)

MINUTES of the [x]th ANNUAL GENERAL MEETING held on Thursday, 24th September 1998 at [address] at 10.00 a.m.

Present: ABC (in the chair)

EFG

HIJ

KLM

NOP

12 shareholders

Apologies for absence were received from QRS, TUV and WXY

In attendance: AAA (Secretary)

BBB (Auditor)

1. Notice

The Secretary read the notice of the meeting (2)

2. Directors Report for the year ended 30th June 1998

The Chairman referred members to the report and accounts for the year ended 30th June 1998 and the balance sheet as at that date. He requested Ms BBB (of accountants – name) to read the audit report which she did. (3)

The Chairman proposed, NOP seconded and it was resolved unanimously that the report and accounts of the company for the year ended 30th June 1998 and the balance sheet as at that date be and they are hereby adopted. (4)

3. Declaration of dividend

The Chairman referred to the payment of an interim dividend in January 1998 and to the fact that the Board were recommending payment of a final dividend of 2p per ordinary shares. He proposed, KLM seconded and it was resolved unanimously that on 25th September 1998, the company should pay a final dividend in respect of the year ended 30th June 1998 of 2p per ordinary share to the holders of ordinary shares registered on the books as at 1st September 1998. (5)

4. Retirement of Directors

The Chairman stated that in accordance with the Articles of Association and as set out in the notice of the meeting, Mrs EFG and Mr KLM retired by rotation and each being eligible, put themselves forward for re-election. The Chairman proposed, Mr HIJ seconded and it was resolved unanimously that the re-election of both retiring Directors could be put to the meeting as one motion. (6)

The Chairman proposed, Mr K Jones, a shareholder seconded, and it was resolved unanimously that Mrs EFG and Mr KLM be and they hereby are re-elected Directors of the company.

5. Auditors

The Chairman referred to the need to re-elect auditors of the company. It was proposed by Mrs EFG, seconded by the Chairman and resolved *nemo contendare* (7) that Messrs [Name] be and they are hereby re-appointed auditors of the company until the conclusion of the next following AGM on terms to be agreed by the Directors.

The meeting terminated at 10.25 a.m.

Chairman .... 26th October 1998...(8)

Notes:

1. Every page should be numbered consecutively. Often Minutes of general and Board Meetings of companies are kept in the same folder and numbered consecutively as one complete record. This can be difficult should a member wish to inspect the Minutes, as members have a right to see the Minutes of general meetings but not of Board Meetings. Thus the Minutes would have to be separated and the

numbering would look somewhat odd unless general meetings Minutes use a prefix and number.

2. There is no requirement to read the notice of the meeting but it can be helpful – if only to give an extra minute or so grace for latecomers to find a seat!

3. Similarly there is no requirement for the auditors to read the audit report (which they will already have had to sign) but again it does little harm and, at the very least, helps identify the auditor to the members.

4. Strictly speaking under common law, when the Chairman proposes a resolution, it is not necessary for him to have a seconder. However, since few members may know this it may be better to arrange seconders. In the interests of democracy it may be better to arrange for seconders to come from shareholders who are not Directors.

5. The members can either approve or reduce the dividend: they cannot increase it. Using a 'striking date' of some time before the meeting should enable all the calculations to be carried out and cheques drawn/credits arranged on the assumption that the dividend will be approved. Once this happens, the payments can be authorised so that members receive them on the due date. PLCs have also to notify the Stock Exchange once a dividend is approved (and indeed to give notice of a Board Meeting at which consideration of a dividend will take place).

6. The re-election of Directors *en masse* can only take place if the meeting has previously approved (as here) that the re-election can take place in this way.

7. *Nemo contendare* means that no one objected to the proposal. Thus, although everyone voted in favour of all the previous proposals, in this instance, whilst no-one voted against, one or more members abstained.

Extraordinary General Meetings

All meetings of the shareholders other than AGMs are Extraordinary General Meetings (EGMs) which need 14 days notice (for guidance regarding the definition of days of notice see page 207). At the AGM envisaged above, only ordinary business was transacted. There is no reason why other business cannot be transacted at the AGM, although the notice would need to reflect such business.

An EGM can be convened by:

- The Board

- Members themselves in accordance with the articles

- Those holding 10 per cent of the members' voting strength

- The auditors, should they resign and feel there are matters which should be brought to the attention of the members, and

- The court.

If the members request the Board to convene an EGM then the Board must do so within 28 days of receiving the members' request and the EGM itself must be convened for a date within a further 21 days (that is the meeting itself must be held within a total of 49 days from the date of the original request).

An EGM only requires 14 days notice, but since the business to be conducted is often out of the ordinary, and resolutions relating to such business may require longer notice in their own right, 21 days notice may be required.

Notice of an EGM can be waived providing 95 per cent of those entitled to attend and vote agree but by passing an elective resolution (which must be filed with the Registrar of Companies), LTD companies can reduce this percentage from 95 per cent to 90 per cent using the elective regime (see later).

Resolutions

The business at a General Meeting is conducted by the shareholders passing (or refusing to pass) resolutions usually set out in full as proposals in the notice of the meeting. There are a number of different types of resolutions and they require different lengths of notice. This is somewhat confusing and the current consultative document regarding changes to Company Law indicates that this is one area which may be simplified. Currently, however, companies have available the range of resolutions set out in the checklist below.

Company resolutions

a) ORDINARY resolution – used to obtain approval by members in General Meetings by means of a simple majority of votes cast. Normally other than recording the decision in the Minutes and implementing it, that is the end of the matter, however, some ordinary resolutions must be filed with the Registrar. These include those that:

  i.   Increase the authorised share capital

  ii. Authorise the Directors to allot shares

  iii. Authorise a voluntarily winding up of the company, and

  iv. Revoke an elective resolution (see below).

b) SPECIAL resolutions are required to:

  i.   Alter the objects clause of the memorandum

  ii. Alter the Articles

  iii. Change the name of the company

  iv. Re-register a private company as a public company, an unlimited company as a limited company, or a public company as a private company

  v.   Disapply pre-emption rights of shareholders (i.e. the rights of shareholders to subscribe for any new shares in the proportion that their existing shareholding bears to the number of shares in issue)

vi. Reduce the company's share capital (which also needs the Court's approval)

vii. Authorise purchase of its own shares or provide assistance to allow purchase of its own shares.

Note: Special resolutions need the approval of 75 per cent of those members entitled to vote present in person or by proxy at a meeting of which 21 days notice has been given.

c) EXTRAORDINARY resolutions are needed to resolve

i. Any matter stated by the articles to require an Extraordinary resolution (unless Company Law now requires it to be subject to the requirements of a Special resolution)

ii. That a company cannot continue in business by reason of its liabilities and should be wound up

iii. To grant certain powers to the liquidator in a members voluntary winding up

iv. That assets of the company in a winding up can be distributed to the members in specie.

Note: Extraordinary resolutions need 14 days notice and the approval of at least 75 per cent of those members entitled to vote present in person or by proxy.

d) SPECIAL NOTICE. In addition to the above the following resolutions require SPECIAL NOTICE (i.e. at least 21 days and the terms to be fully stated)

i. Any resolution relating to an auditor other than for the re-election of an auditor elected at the previous AGM or to settle his remuneration

ii. The removal of a Director, or (for PLCs and subsidiaries of PLCs only) the appointment or re-election as a Director of such a company of a Director aged 70 or over.

e) For PRIVATE COMPANIES only there are two relaxations to the rules:

- WRITTEN RESOLUTIONS: If ALL members sign and return a copy of a resolution, then the resolution will be passed notwithstanding that the members have not gathered in one place. The effective date of the resolution is the date the last copy is signed and once signed it must be recorded in the Minute Book. This written process cannot be used for resolutions removing Directors or auditors.

- ELECTIVE RESOLUTIONS: If having been given 21 days notice and ALL members entitled to attend and vote at a General Meeting agree, then private companies can pass resolutions to:

    i. Give or renew Director's authority to allot shares

    ii. Dispense with laying of accounts before a meeting (in this case the accounts must be sent to each member with the proposed elective resolution)

    iii. Dispense with the holding of an AGM

    iv. Reduce the percentage required for sanctioning short notice of EGM from 95 per cent to 90 per cent, and

    v. Dispense with annual re-appointment of auditors (in which case the auditors are deemed to be automatically re-elected.

All elective resolutions must be filed with the Registrar as must any resolution (ordinary) revoking them. Should a private company re-register as a public company all elective resolutions are automatically void.

Summary checklist

✓ The AGM is a public showing of the corporate body and needs to proceed smoothly – attention to detail is essential.

✓ Required notice of General Meetings must be given taking account of 'non service' days.

✓ A timetable of items with those responsible should be compiled.

✓ A brief should be provided for 'first time' Chairman to ensure the event goes smoothly.

✓ Minutes must be prepared and made available at the Registered Office for inspection by shareholders.

✓ The use of and requirements of support for the various types of shareholder resolutions need to be fully understood and the Articles referred to for any special requirements.

chapter twelve

Going public

Aspects of the PLC requirement

Corporate re-registration

Most companies start life as private companies – often with a tiny share capital (say £100 nominal) and only two shareholders (each holding one share). If the company is profitable, its assets start to accumulate and, assuming the owners wish the company to continue to grow, part of these profits can be retained – possibly with additional shares issued in respect of the additional value created. Alternatively, fresh capital may be introduced evidenced by additional shares being issued. There is usually a limit to the amount of capital that can be acquired either by the retention of profits and/or by introducing new capital from relatives and friends of the first Directors and/or shareholders. If substantial additional capital is required it may be necessary for the Directors to consider a public flotation – i.e. offering shares on the capital market operated by the Stock Exchange either for public subscription or by subscription through contacts of a broker (a share placing, which has the advantage that to some extent, at least initially, the company can choose its shareholders).

Ignoring the mechanics of the share issue itself, for a private (LTD) company to become a public (PLC) the formalities set out in the checklist below must be observed

Re-registration LTD to PLC

a) The company needs to change its name to end in 'Public Limited Company' or 'PLC' (instead of Limited or LTD) by the passing of a special resolution) and to alter its Memorandum (i.e. to reflect the name change and any alteration regarding the amount of share capital).

b) The company may also need to change its Articles (again by resolution of the shareholders) to remove any restriction on the number of members the company may have and the Directors rights to refuse a share transfer. (Many LTD companies restrict the total number of shareholders and give Directors considerable powers to refuse to register new shareholders.)

c) Form 43 plus the amended Memorandum re the change of name together with:

- A statement from Auditors that the net assets of the company exceed the sum of the paid up share capital and undistributable reserves (as defined in section 264 of Companies Act 1985)

- A balance sheet made up to a date not more than seven months prior to the re-registration application with an unqualified auditors report, and

- A statutory declaration made by a Director or the Company Secretary

must be filed with the Registrar of Companies.

d) The company must obtain a certificate of re-registration on change of name.

e) The company must ensure it meets the requirements regarding paid up share capital – it must have a share capital of at least £50,000 of which 25 per cent must be paid up and received – and this must be confirmed by the auditors to the Registrar. If the value of the shares is to be met by a consideration other than cash then 'receipt' of this value must be confirmed.

Following the submission of the items referred to above, when the Registrar is satisfied, a certificate to commence trading will be issued. Until the receipt of this certificate the company must not trade as a PLC – if it does the Directors responsible are in breach of Company Law and liable to fine etc.

Note: Any elective resolutions (e.g. not to hold an AGM – see Chapter 11) passed by the company when it was an LTD cease to be effective once it becomes a PLC.

WARNING: A company can be a plc without being listed on the Stock Exchange.

....

For the sake of completeness it may be appropriate at this point to record the requirements should a PLC wish to revert to being an LTD and these requirements are set out in the checklist below:

Re-registration PLC to LTD

a) The company must change its name (by means of a special resolution) so that it ends in LIMITED or LTD and must alter its Memorandum to evidence the name change and must also resolve to re-register as an LTD company.

b) The company may need to change its Articles.

c) Form 54 with an altered copy of Memorandum and Articles must be filed with the Registrar.

....

Public flotation and the implications

As noted above in order to expand, businesses need capital, and LTDs traditionally source this from:

- The founders/owners

- Family and personal contacts

- Banks and money lending organisations (e.g. factors, etc.)

But once these sources have been tapped may need to access the capital markets to obtain funds from:

- Third party individual investors

- Institutional investors

- The international money market.

A public flotation has both advantages and disadvantages.

Flotation implications

Advantages

1. A Stock Exchange listing grants a prestige to the company. In itself it may be able to avoid Directors needing to give personal guarantees, provide an edge in negotiations, assistance in obtaining further finance, etc.

2. Subject to its trading performance, a listed company possesses a capacity to issue additional shares thereby generating more capital – on which, if it is equity capital, the return (i.e. dividends) can be restricted in poor years. In addition the company should have easier access to the non-equity capital market (i.e. fixed-interest bearing securities).

3. As far as the existing shareholders are concerned, the drawback of investing in a private company is removed as a market exists to allow trading in the shares. Owners can time their withdrawal to match market buoyancy.

Perceived adverse factors

1. Full disclosure of all the activities of the company (and its officers) must occur, particularly where the company has a high consumer profile. Because of the effect of loss of confidence on the share price, such disclosure needs to be handled very carefully.

2. It is not just the media and the analysts who will be aware of the company – so too will be the consumer. Adverse publicity can affect the attractiveness of the sector/company and thus the attractiveness of the shares.

3. Few companies exist without competition and thus attention to the sector may generate individual company attention, even though the comments may not apply to individual companies. Preparation to defend a position and promote awareness of the true position is essential.

4. Being in the public eye and being part of a sector, companies are judged by reference to their peer group (despite the obvious imperfections of this). In addition, due to the pressure put on institutional investors, pressure (both latent and actual) is brought to bear on public companies to perform. This may have the effect of forcing the creation of enhanced short-term profits albeit at the expense of longer term development, training, experimentation etc.

5. The shares of public companies become commodities. Different viewpoints may emerge between those we can call share investors (principally institutions many of whom will seek shorter term gains from trading in the company's and other companies shares) and shareholders (predominantly private shareholders most of whom tend to hold the shares on a long-term basis). The former may seek to make shorter term gains out of an investment which is really geared to long-term holding. The latter tend to act as a homogeneous mass and may, if there is a hostile bid, tend to support the company – if only through inactivity.

6. The activities of the company, as well as its results, may become subject to strict attention, the focus of which depends as much on social comment and pressure as on profitability.

Application for Stock Exchange listing

For the detailed requirements for a public flotation, reference should be made to the latest edition of the Stock Exchange's *Admission of Securities* to listing (a loose-leaf updated manual commonly called the Yellow Book because of the colour of its folder) although the main principles are set out in the checklist below:

Application for listing requirements

A company must:

- Be an established business with a five year record of trading with unqualified opinion on its results given by the reporting auditors

- Have adequate management skills and systems

- Be prepared to make a minimum of 25 per cent of its shares available to the public

- Have an expected market capitalisation of £700,000

- Expect to achieve annual pre-tax profits of at least £1M

- Issue a prospectus

- Undertake to comply with the obligations contained in the *Admission of Securities* to listing book and the *City Code on Takeovers* (the blue book).

In addition listed companies are subject to a number of continuing requirement including:

- The provision of all information necessary to enable holders of the company's listed securities and the public to appraise the position of the company and to avoid the creation of a false market in the securities. The principle behind a listing is that all those dealing in the shares should have the same information

- Application to list new shares of a class already listed must be made not more than a month before listing.

- All holders of the same shares must receive equal treatment with existing holders having rights of pre-emption

  (Note: Rights of pre-emption – i.e. that new shares must be offered to existing shareholders in the proportion their shares bear to the total in issue – are often voted away in General Meeting.)

- Companies wishing to raise money find a sponsor – typically a merchant bank. Share issues of up to £25 million can be placed entirely with the clients of the sponsor. For issues over £25 million and under £50 million, shares can be sold partly by placing and partly by an offer for sale. Shares with a value of £50 million or more must be marketed to the public

- The company must notify all information which would have a material effect on the price of its shares

- The date of any Board Meeting at which a dividend may be decided, or at which profits(losses) for any period, are to be approved, must be notified by the company at least ten days in advance. Any decision taken at the meeting must then be notified to the Stock Exchange immediately

- Any Board decision regarding a change of the capital structure or redemption of listed securities, or a change in the rights of any listed security of the company, must be notified immediately

- Depending on the percentage of value of the assets being changed (e.g. disposed of) to the total assets, the company must provide a range of information

- All matters concerning the interests of Directors (including the interest of any spouse and/or infant children) in the securities of the company, must be notified immediately. Within 14 days of appointment Directors are required to submit formal statements of past and present business activities. A statement must be made of the possible liability should a Director's service contract be broken

- Should the company wish to purchase its own shares and the Board wish to submit a resolution to this effect before a General Meeting, then that decision, and the decision of the meeting, when held, must be notified immediately

(Note: The possibility of the rules regarding such share purchases being relaxed is being reviewed by the DTI.)

- Where a shareholder owns or acquires a holding of three per cent or more in the company securities, or changes such holding by one per cent or more, the company must be informed and it must notify the Stock Exchange forthwith. In addition, anyone who holds shares by means of what are called non-material holdings must also disclose their interest if the aggregate of such material and non-material interests reach or exceed ten per cent

- An annual report and accounts must be issued within six months of the end of the financial period. Such accounts are subject to detailed requirements, for example:

    a) If the company has subsidiaries consolidated group accounts must be published

    b) Any significant departure from standard accounting practices must be stated

    c) Results which differ materially from any published forecast made by the company must be explained

    d) A geographical analysis of turnover and profits of non-UK operations must be provided

e) Details of each subsidiary in which the company has an interest of 20 per cent or more in the equity must be given

f) A detailed analysis of borrowings in terms of up to one year, one to two years, two to five years and five years or more, must be provided

g) The interests of the Directors (including spouses and infant children) in the shares (including options) of the company and any changes during the year must be given

h) The material interest of any shareholder holding in excess of three per cent of the equity capital and the non-material interest of any shareholder controlling in excess of ten per cent, and any interest which in aggregate (material and non-material) exceeds ten per cent must be stated.

i) Whether the company is a close company (i.e. all its shares are owned by the Directors, or of five or less members) must be stated

j) Any contract in which any Director is interested must be stated

k) Particulars of any contract between the company (or a subsidiary) and a substantial corporate shareholder must be given

l) Details of shareholders authority for the purchase by the company of its own shares must be provided, and

m) The identity of independent non-executive Directors with biographical notes on each must be given.

In addition to the above application and continuing obligations a listed company must also comply with a number of administrative requirements.

Stock Exchange
administrative requirements

A company must:

a) Have one (or more) brokers to represent the company

b) File six copies of every circular sent to shareholders with each Stock Exchange on which it is listed

c) Ensure its Directors comply with the model code, including not trading in the company's shares for two months prior to the announcement of any results or of the publication of information likely to affect the price of its shares. The aim of this restriction is to try to prevent abuse of knowledge – i.e. to restrict insider dealing

d) Notify all changes in the Directorate or changes in office

e) Make available copies of all Directors' service contracts of more than a year (or a written résumé if the contract is not in writing) for inspection at the registered office or transfer office during usual business hours between the date of the notice of the AGM and the date of the AGM, and for at least 15 Minutes prior to the AGM. The potential liability should the contract be terminated must be stated

f) State that such contracts are available for inspection during that time in the notice of the meeting

g) Provide details, in the case of any Director whose re-election will be considered at the AGM, of the unexpired portion of such service contract in the Directors' report.

Notification of major interests

Any shareholder who holds three per cent or more of the issued shares is required to advise the company of the fact. The company must then immediately notify the Exchange. Each time the holding varies by one per cent (up or down) further notifications are required.

In addition those with a non-material interest (e.g. an interest as a Trustee for a beneficiary who is the ultimate holder) of ten per cent or more (or who have material and non-material interests which in aggregate reach or exceed ten per cent) must also notify the company and be notified to the Stock Exchange.

Not all holders use their own names to control the shares, and to negate the effect of the shareholder trying to hide behind a false name, under Section 212 of the Companies Act, a company can require the shareholder to disclose the name of the holder (see draft below).

If the company serves such a notice the shareholder can be obliged to reply within two days. The identity of the actual shareholder(s) (i.e. not any nominee names) with three per cent of the shares or more must be stated in the Directors report in the Annual Report.

Draft Section 212 notice

(Request to be served on the shareholder notified, if the company suspects the name in which the shares are held is not the name of the real shareholder.)

To: Shareholders name and address

Subject: Interest in [company] shares

Pursuant to section 212 of the Companies Act 1985, we require you to provide us with the following information in writing (or by telex, fax or electronic transmission) within [number] days of the date of this letter (i.e. by [date])

    a)   The number of shares in which you have an interest in this company as at the date of your reply (your current interest) and the number of shares in which you have had an interest at any time in the last [up to three maximum] years preceding the date of this notice (your past interest)

b) The nature of your interest in the above shares

c) The date(s) when you acquired and/or disposed of the shares

d) The full name and address of each person who has an interest in those shares together with particulars of the interest and the number of shares in which each person had an interest

e) Details of any agreement or arrangement relating to the exercise of any voting or other rights applying to the shares in which you have or had an interest, together with the names and addresses of each party to any such agreement or arrangement

Yours etc.

Note: Should a shareholder not comply with the request for information then the company may disenfranchise the shares. Companies considering this action should discuss the proposals first with the Stock Exchange. The Exchange does not encourage disenfranchising shares since it can have the effect of shares with different rights being in circulation.

Corporate governance

A company listed on the stock exchange must sign a copy of the listing agreement which entails Directors undertaking to comply with it. These listing agreement obligations are developing as a result of the deliberations of the Cadbury, Greenbury and Hampel committees on Corporate Governance.

The supercode which incorporates the recommendations of all three committees was published in July 1998. Listed PLCs are requested to comply voluntarily.

The Cadbury code of best practice

Board should:

- Meet regularly, control the company and monitor management

- Ensure a distinction between the roles of Chairman and Chief Executive to ensure a balance of power (if the roles are combined there should be a strong independent – non-executive – presence on the Board)

- Appoint non-executive Directors capable of exerting power

- Prepare and adhere to a schedule of matters for consideration – arrange for Directors to take independent professional advice at the expense of the company and to have access to the Company Secretary

- Discuss as a body any question of the removal of the Company Secretary.

Non-executive Directors should:

- Bring an independent judgement in Board matters

- Include a majority who can act independently, free from any relationship which might interfere with their judgement

- Be appointed for a set term without automatic reselection

- Be appointed formally by the whole Board.

Executive Directors should:

- Not be granted service contracts in excess of three years duration without shareholders' approval

- Ensure their pay is subject to the deliberations of a remuneration committee comprised wholly or partly of non-executive Directors

- Disclose clearly and fully their total emoluments as well as the actual figures for the Chairman and highest paid Director providing separate figures for salary and performance related elements.

Reporting:

- The Board must exercise its responsibility to present a balanced and understandable assessment of the company's position, utilising an objective and professional relationship with the auditors and acknowledging this responsibility in a note in the accounts adjacent to the audit report

- An audit committee (see below) should be established comprising mainly non-executive Directors

- The Board should report on the effectiveness of the company's system of control and on the basis of a going concern with supporting assumptions or qualifications as necessary.

An audit committee might examine the following:

- Any change in accounting policies and the reasons for the change, and that such policies are most appropriate for the company

- Any reservations indicated by the auditors concerning the accounting policies or their implementation or interpretation

- Issues raised in the audit management letter

- Compliance by the accounts with latest standards

- Material changes from estimates included in previous accounts or statements

- The effect of all known contingencies and material events being adequately reflected in the accounts

- That disclosures have been made of all relevant party transactions

- That the accounts disclose the effect of any and all acquisitions and disposals and any contingent liabilities including outstanding litigation

- That interim accounts have been prepared in accordance with similar processes and policies as used at the year end, updated as necessary

- Compliance with changes in standards, law and/or Stock Exchange regulations

- Relationship between the company and professional advisers.

Obviously Directors and Secretaries of public companies need to be aware of the latest requirements in this area. This however may not absolve Directors of LTD companies from being similarly aware since it is possible that some of the requirements suggested by those committees may be replicated in a future Companies Act although this is not the current intention of the Government. In its document commencing the consultative process that will eventually lead to the creation of a new Companies Act, the DTI refers to the deliberations of these committees and the creation of the supercode (see above) as being more appropriate to best practice rather than legislation. However, the document goes on to state that 'there may however be a need for legislation in certain areas which are not covered by the new code or where experience shows that some legal underpinning is needed' and suggests the following areas for further legislation:

- The duties of Directors: where it is suggested that the Government should 'clarify Directors' duties to take a broader view of their responsibilities' which could include the interests of other parties such as employees, creditors, customers, the environment and the wider community (although as already noted there are already existing obligations on Directors to take account of most of these interests)

- The conduct of General Meetings: where changes might be aimed at enabling shareholders to play a more active role in their companies

- Shareholder control over Directors' pay.

Payment of Directors

Considerable attention has been focussed in recent years on the question of Directors pay not least since there are a number of well-recorded instances where Directors, particularly of former nationalised industries continuing to operate in a virtual monopolistic situation have awarded themselves substantially increased salaries and benefits. It may of course have been the case that the previous levels of pay were inappropriate and the new levels are commensurate with changed responsibilities but the fact remains that the increases have seldom been handled appropriately and with adequate explanation. In one case a massive increase for the Managing Director was announced at the same time as 2000 redundancies. Whilst both decisions may have been correct the juxtaposition of the announcements must call into question the quality of management of the company failing to anticipate the outcry that followed. Unfortunately we live in a society where relatively few 'performers' in the entertainment business (including the sporting field) can command very large payments even though they have relatively little responsibility. Compared with such earnings, the amount we pay those who control our wealth-creating companies and who carry considerable and far greater responsibilities as well as laying themselves open to the liabilities referred to earlier, may not be at all disproportionate.

Nevertheless, in the UK there seems to be a far wider gap between the earnings of those who direct companies and those at the sharp end who carry out their instructions. It is not impossible to imagine a situation where a company could simply adopt a widely known multiplier which, when applied to the earnings of the sharp end employee, would generate the maximum payable to the Managing Director. Thus, if the average salary of the shop floor operative was £15,000 and the multiplier was 20 the maximum salary of the MD would be £300,000. Inevitably as the 'worth' of those on the shop floor rose as a result of market pressures so too would that of the Managing Director. Such a concept need only be a guideline but divergence from such a norm would require explanation which itself would force objective justification of top people's pay.

Summary
checklist

✓ The detailed requirements and implications of re-registration need to be assessed prior to taking such a step.

✓ Full advice should be taken before considering a public flotation and the requirements of the listing agreement and the continuing obligations appreciated.

✓ All major interests (i.e. of three per cent or any change resulting in a whole percentage figure alteration) in shares must be recorded and notified to the Stock Exchange on which the shares are quoted.

✓ Public listed companies need to comply with the supercode of Corporate Governance, or need to state in their Annual Report which items they have not complied with.

chapter thirteen

'Write a better book'

Shareholder communication

The Annual Report

'If a man write a better book... the world will make a beaten path to his door'. Ralph Waldo Emerson's 100 year old dictum might still be useful guidance to those responsible for modern corporate literature which often it must be said leaves a great deal to be desired in terms of clarity and a genuine wish to inform. Directors are required to give account of their stewardship of the assets placed under their control to their shareholders and specifically must provide them with:

- The company's financial results and accounts (and explanatory notes thereto) for the previous financial period

- A balance sheet as at the end of the period, and

- A report of the Directors on the financial period and any material facts since its close.

As well as reporting this data to the shareholders, such data must also be filed with the Registrar of Companies. The contents of these items are prescribed by law, and accounting practice (which has the authority of law). Although the Directors are required to include in their report a résumé of the company's activities in the period under review, this tends to be supplemented by a far longer and more descriptive statement usually under the name of the Chairman or Chief Executive. In fact there is no legal requirement for a company to publish a Chairman's statement but most listed public companies and many unlisted ones do publish this as part of the document that is usually known as an Annual Report. For most private companies the Annual Report will be a fairly simple document concentrating primarily on the financial results. However, for listed companies the report is regarded as a document of record and a chance to promote the corporate entity. As a result many such documents tend to resemble glossy brochures. Sadly, although many may find the illustrations of interest the presentation of financial and other information leaves much to be desired. So complex have the reporting requirements become, that the interests of the average reader seem to be subsumed in a mass of data. As the Institute of Chartered Accountants' *Report on Summary Financial Statements* (see below) comments:

> 'We believe that the complexity of modern accounting disclosures militates against clarity of communication',

whilst the Institute of Chartered Accountants of Scotland commented in its book '*Making corporate reports valuable*'

> 'Present-day financial statements are often almost incomprehensible to anyone other than their preparers'.

Sadly such comments are borne out by surveys of report readers.

Shareholders' views of the Annual Report

- 23 per cent of shareholders stated they had not received their company's Annual Report (since Royal Mail state that less than two per cent of posted items 'go astray', one is tempted to wonder if so little did the report appeal to most of the 23 per cent that they could not remember having received it!):

- 18 per cent said they read none of it

- 24 per cent said they 'glanced through it'

- 15 per cent said they read 'some of it'

- 11 per cent said they read 'most of it' and

- only 9 per cent said they read 'all of it'.

  Source: MORI

If a score of 20 per cent reading most or all of such reports were not low enough, a study of comprehension levels was carried out by the London Business School and Wolff Olins/Hall. The study revealed that 75 per cent of those who claimed to have read their company's reports stated that they understood them. However, when they were tested, only a third displayed a 'reasonable grasp' of the contents. If only 20 per cent of the total audience actually read reports and of the 75 per cent of them who claimed to understand them, only a third displayed a reasonable grasp, this suggests that only around five per cent of the original audience actually understood the documents. Other comments made in the London Business School survey were that the reports were too 'stodgy and technical', whilst only 40 per cent of the audience identified any part of the report as being 'particularly informative'. If new Company Law is aimed at increasing shareholders interest in and control over the activities of their companies, it seems there is an urgent need to encourage more constructive and intelligible financial reporting – not least since if Emerson is correct, companies which produce a better 'corporate book' might find the world beating a path to their door – which is unlikely to be bad for business!

Determining the target audiences

In considering preparing the 'corporate book' the following provides an outline guide to the task, the first consideration being the identification of its target audiences:

Audience for Annual Report

1. Shareholders – private, institutional and prospective

2. Stock Exchanges

3. Analysts

4. Mailing list

5. Advisers, brokers, media

6. Government agencies, local and national politicians

7. Accounting professions

8. Creditors, lenders, developers, customers, landlords etc.

9. Employees (current and retired)

10. Recruitment agencies, schools and universities

11. Trades unions

12. Pressure groups

13. Archivists and libraries

14. Competitors.

Note: Whether intended for them or not competitors are likely to obtain a copy, so care needs to be exercised regarding confidentiality of products, processes etc.

Given the difficulties of communicating meaningfully to those that actually have money invested in the company, it may be impossible to satisfy all the audiences but at least identifying them may help consideration of the holistic nature of the document. It may also focus attention on the need to make the document more understandable to those who are not financially orientated.

Filing the document

All companies are required to file their results with the Registrar of Companies within a strict timetable – by the end of seven months after the year end for public companies, and by the end of ten months for private companies (although both can gain an extension of three months to these time limits if they have one or more overseas subsidiaries whose results are required to be consolidated with the results of UK companies).

Reporting results, however, is not simply a matter of complying with statutory requirements. Business is about confidence and, particularly for a public listed company, the reporting of results is an important facet of the building and sustaining of confidence. The tone, quality and presentation of the Annual Report says a great deal about the company and for this reason, amongst others, great care needs to be exercised when considering the timing and execution of statements concerning the company's achievements. It is for this reason that all those who may wish to see the report should be listed and their requirements considered. This does not mean the report must be all things to all men – the prime function is to report to the shareholders. However in preparing a report there is no reason why, if it is felt appropriate, the interests of other audiences should not also be addressed. In this the aim may be more corporate promotion than company reporting but there is no reason why Directors should not use one document to serve two purposes – indeed it may be cost-effective to do so. Why not encourage the use of the Annual Report as a means of corporate promotion – at least if it has this aim there will be more pressure on those who create such reports to make them readable and their content accessible?

Range of content

Companies are legally bound to include within their Annual Report a range of items including the items set out in the checklist below.

Required items to be included

- Accounts and balance sheet plus explanatory notes as required under Company Law, required standards of accounting practice and (if applicable) the Stock Exchange listing agreement

- Auditor's report

- Report of the Directors – this must include – a statement of the principal activities of the company

- A review of the development of the business in the period

- Details of developments since the year end and any anticipated developments

- Details of research and development

- Transfers to reserves

- Profit, and retained profit, after dividend payment

- Dividends paid and proposed

- Significant changes of assets

- Own share acquisition or disposal

- Details of Directors throughout the period and of their shareholdings at the beginning and end of the period

- Details of shareholdings totalling or exceeding three per cent (and non-material holdings totalling or exceeding ten per cent in aggregate)

- Political and charitable donations

- Information concerning the employment of disabled persons and of action taken to consult and involve employees (for companies whose average workforce exceeds 250)

- Information concerning the arrangements re health, safety and welfare of employees.

The Directors' report must be approved by the Board and signed on its behalf by a Director or the Secretary. It must then be laid before the company in General Meeting and then filed with the Registrar with the accounts and balance sheet within the specified time limits. Although many companies require their shareholders to approve the report and accounts in fact there is no requirement to gain shareholder approval and even if the shareholders reject the items, they are still the report and accounts of the company for that period and as such can and must be filed with the Registrar.

Theme

Although the legally required items cannot be changed, the relative importance of the aims and audiences of an individual report will vary both from company to company and within the same company from time to time. The aggressive conglomerate growing by acquisition may normally wish to use a high profile image, although conversely at times it may need to 'dampen things down' whilst secretively stalking a particular prey. The High Street chain store may have (and wish to sustain) a higher awareness profile than a similar-sized manufacturing company. The newer 'high-tech' industries tend to have a higher profile than the older, more established companies, and so on.

The relative importance of each aim needs to be assessed and built into a theme to which constant reference should be made to ensure the impression given by each item (particularly if these are written by several authors) is consistent, and that illustrations and pictorial inserts similarly reflect the same 'message'.

Style

There are and can be no hard and fast rules concerning the design of corporate communications, other than the fact that the style of communication should reflect the style of each individual company at that particular stage of its development. Above all, however, a report should (and many fail) to seek to EXPLAIN the results and the strategy in simple everyday language – and this aim of explanation should be tested from time to time by surveying the audience.

As noted above far too many corporate reports leave all but the qualified accountant numb with incomprehension and the private shareholder, perhaps understandably, somewhat annoyed that a considerable amount of company resources has been devoted to producing what they perceive to be a largely unintelligible document. Research has suggested that many private shareholders gain most of their appreciation of the progress of their company and of the salient features of the results, by reading an Employee Report (see below) rather than by studying the Annual Report. In preparing an Employee Report, simplified in content for a non-financially aware audience, the editor is forced, if only by lack of space, to concentrate on the salient features and general trends rather than the mass of detail which can tend to obscure the important central messages in an Annual Report.

Writing with the awareness that the target audience may not be largely financially aware helps the best of such reports to achieve admirable clarity. However, it is often overlooked that the overwhelming majority of number (if not of shareholding) of the target audience of most Annual Reports may be non-financially expert. Both in writing and in presentation, clarity and lucidity should be watchwords.

A timetable for action

Planning

Whilst the following timetable attempts to address all situations, it is provided merely as a draft and needs to be customised to satisfy individual needs. In some companies the overall responsibility may be that of the Financial Director rather than, as envisaged here, that of the Company Secretary, either of whom may in turn delegate much of the detail to a designer.

Whether the Chairman (and other executives) write their own statements or have them (or at least an initial draft) written by the Company Secretary or a professional ghost-writer also needs to be determined.

Since the Annual Report of most public listed companies incorporates the Notice of the Annual General Meeting the Company Secretary will need to relate all requirements in that regard – booking the venue, arranging the event, ensuring the report is posted and gives sufficient notice, etc. – to this timetable.

Timetable for
Annual Report production

THE TIMETABLE		(D = Despatch date)
Item	**Timing**	**Executive(s)**
Prepare budget	D – 100	Comp.Sec./ Fin. Dir.
Prepare timetable (in liaison with ghostwriter/ designer/typesetters/ printers)	D – 90	Comp.Sec./ Fin. Dir.
Rough mock-up of report	D – 80	Designer/Fin. Dir
Board agree budget and mock-up		Board
Chairman's statement 1st draft		Ghostwriter/ Chairman
Executives' reports 1st draft		[Initials]
Proxy and other cards (e.g. AGM attendance and admittance cards) 1st draft		Comp. Sec.
Chairman's statement, etc. 2nd draft	D – 80	Ghostwriter/ Chairman
Analyse number of reports required	D – 70	Comp. Sec.

Advise printer so that paper can be ordered		Comp. Sec.
Photographer/illustrator commissioned and instructed		Designer/ Comp. Sec.
Chairman's statement, final draft and copy to printers/typesetters	D – 60	Ghostwriter/ Chairman
Liaise with registrars and provide checklist	D – 50	Comp. Sec.
Liaise with corporate public relations		
Liaise with brokers		
First proof back, checked and returned to typesetters		Comp.Sec./Auditors
Second proof to company/auditors	D – 40	Comp.Sec./Auditors
Photographs/illustrations reviewed and agreed		Chairman
Third proof (colour)	D – 30	Comp.Sec./Auditors
Preliminary announcement	D – 25	Comp.Sec.
Insert figures in third proof for typesetters		Comp.Sec.
Commission dividend warrants		Comp.Sec.
Final proof checked	D – 15	Chairman/Comp.Sec.
Print order given. Printers liaise with registrars to collect envelopes and despatch	D – 10	Printers/Comp.Sec.

Report despatched externally	D – 1	Despatch
Report distributed internally	D – day	Comp.Sec.

The Chairman's statement

In many respects the statement by the Chairman or Chief Executive is the key item in the report and the main item of commentary and information for the owners of the business. There is no legal requirement to include such a statement although its omission from a listed company's report would generate adverse comments. Indeed given the fact that little of an Annual Report seems to be read and understood by 95 per cent of the target audience it would be regrettable if the one part of the report that is likely to be read was not available to put flesh on the 'bare bones' provided by the figures. In addition, whereas the remainder of the report considers past events – some as much as 18 months old – such a statement is the one item that can, as well as explaining reasons, strategy, etc., actually look forward – a view likely to be of greater interest to most investors. However, views of the future tend to be couched in generalistic and wide terms (see below).

Approach

The type of statement will very much depend on the personality of the Chairmen and on the 'attitude' adopted by the company at the time of writing.

Style and content for a Chairman's statement

Style

- Establish impression to be given (e.g. forward looking, high quality performance, retrenching, expansionist, etc.)

- Adhere to a theme and (if supporting reports are written by a number of executives) ensure this theme is repeated in individual reports (which may require some editing of other's reports)

- Provide reassurance and confidence (but only if that view is supportable)

- Give an indication of progress (or explanation of reason for lack of progress)

- Endeavour to bolster prestige and reputation if applicable.

Content

The statement should include:

- Brief résumé of the salient financial data (sales, profit, dividend, amount reinvested) in each case possibly compared with the figures for the previous year, although if any show decreases it may be preferable for the comparable figure to be omitted

- Commentary on trading (and sometimes general economic/political) conditions and how the company has reacted to them. This may be expanded either within the Chairman's statement itself so that each division within the organisation is featured (possibly even with individual results) or may form part of a separate 'divisional' review which may incorporate photos etc.

- Acquisitions and disposals (at least those of any significance)

- Explanation of exceptional items (i.e. those that are outside the normal business activities)

- Trade investments

- Adherence to (or deviation from) required corporate governance requirements

- Board changes, employee details, training etc.

- Product development and launches (where these can be discussed publicly)

- The trading strategy for the immediate future (again where this can be discussed publicly)

   WARNING: In fact any comments on this last subject are likely to be given only in general terms as most Chairmen will be wary about giving 'hostages to fortune' in their statements. For this reason this part of the statement tends to feature somewhat bland and generalised comments rather than being precise. Chairmen of PLCs particularly need to be careful not to include what could be construed as a 'profit forecast' and the advice of the auditors or legal advisers may need to be sought.

Checking history

When drafting a statement, care needs to be taken to check what is already on record as no Chairman will relish being 'caught out' (particularly when answering questions at the AGM and/or posed by the media) because something in a later report contradicts, without adequate explanation, a comment or policy previously on record. In preparing the statement, the comments need to be placed in context and the author (whether the Chairman or another internal or external ghostwriter) needs to refer to items such as those set out in the following checklist:

The existing record

The content of the following items need to be checked:

- The Chairman's previous two or three Statements

- The Interim Statement

- Any press releases and comments made at annual or other meetings

- Any interviews or observations made by the Chairman

- The results and developments of the business and any strategy adopted by the Board

- Any press or other comment made on the company and/or its products (in case criticism can be answered and/or the record corrected).

Other documentation

Summary Financial Statement

In place of the full Annual Report, companies may now send to their shareholders a summary statement. A Summary Financial Statement (SFS) must be consistent with the full accounts and the auditors are required to certify that this is so. The SFS must state whether the Auditor's Report on the full accounts was qualified or not.

Required content of SFS

- Key section of the Director's Report:
  - business review
  - post balance sheet events
  - future developments
  - Director's details.

- Summary profit and loss account containing:

  - pre-tax profit/loss for financial period

  - tax and post-tax profit

  - extraordinary and exceptional items

  - dividends paid and proposed

  - Directors payments.

- Summary balance sheet showing:

  - issued share capital

  - reserves

  - provisions

  - liabilities and assets

  - contingent liabilities.

- Auditor's report.

To discover whether shareholders would prefer to have the SFS, companies must first either:

- Send both summary statement and full report to their shareholders with a reply paid card, stating that unless the shareholder indicates, he will in future only be sent the summary version, or

- Canvas their shareholders in advance to discover who wishes to receive the summary version.

The interim report

Listed PLCs are required to produce an interim report – usually as at a date six months into their financial period although some companies produce quarterly interims. Either such a report must be sent out or the company can advertise its results in two national newspapers. In either case the information must be supplied not later than four months after the end of the period. Interim statements do not have to be audited but most auditors may wish to at least review the figures.

The preliminary announcement

As soon as the results for the full year are known a listed PLC company is required to publish a Preliminary Announcement giving the salient details. This tends to be published around three months after the year end with the Annual Report published up to a month later. Any price reactions of the shares will tend to be made in response to the information contained in the Preliminary and strict confidentiality must surround its generation.

Employee Reports

There is no legal requirement to produce an Employee Report but around 200 listed PLCs do so, as do a larger number of other organisations. The best of such reports tend to be successful because they are relatively unconstrained by legal requirements, although there is a requirement, often ignored, for such reports to contain a statement that the figures are an extract from the full Report and Accounts which have been lodged with the Registrar of Companies (S255, Companies Act 1985).

Unfettered by legal requirements, employee reports can provide a clear and instant guide to the overall trend of the business and, for this reason, private shareholders, in particular, value as such the best of such reports. Research has shown that where such reports are sent to shareholders, often much of the information retained by the shareholders has been derived from reading the employee report rather than the Annual Report.

The following checklist of contents should be used as a guide from which perhaps a majority of the items should be selected for inclusion. The need is to produce a report which **explains** the salient features and significance of the results.

Suggested content for Employee Report

a) Statements of the aims of the business and of the report

b) Specially composed statement (i.e. not a reprint of the statement in the Annual Report) by the Chairman or Managing Director (in ordinary English which avoids jargon)

c) Highlights of the year (i.e. clearly indicating progress – or lack of same)

d) Balance sheet (with an explanation of the terms used)

e) Simplified Profit & Loss a/c or Added Value statement

f) Statement of sales and profit, particularly expressed on a per employee and/or a localised or divisional basis. (If inflation is high it may help show real growth by adjusting for inflation.)

g) General information regarding products or services, employees, share schemes, environmental and community matters, etc.

h) Organisation charts

i) Comment on future plans or developments

j) Graphics and illustrations supporting and complementing the above items.

Note: Since most readers 'minds' eyes' can capture trends and proportions far more easily if expressed in graphic form than in a line or list of figures/text, the use of clear user-friendly graphics should help achieve better reader comprehension.

(from *'Financial Reporting to Employees – a practical guide'*, David Martin)

Letter of welcome

An increasing number of listed PLCs write to new shareholders welcoming their investment and setting out the financial calendar of the company. There is no requirement to issue such a letter but it can create a rapport between new shareholder and company. There may be other matters that the Board would like to indicate to the shareholder – urging them to attend the AGM, details of any discount scheme, payment of dividends by direct transfer rather than by warrant and so on.

Letter of invitation to the AGM (and other General Meetings)

The notice of General Meetings tends to be included in the Annual Report and as such, often because space is limited, may be fairly formal. Some companies have amplified the formal notice with such a letter from the Chairman, particularly if there are matters other than the routine business to be considered at the meeting. The letter can explain the reasons behind proposals which could, for example, have the result of gaining support where none might otherwise have been forthcoming.

Admission card

Companies with large numbers of shareholders tend to issue admission cards bearing their name, the number of shares etc. If a shareholder attends the meeting without such a card they cannot be barred from entering but the production of the card simply aids the admission formalities.

Summary checklist

✓ The person responsible for the compilation of the Annual Report must consider the requirements of the target audience and write the report accordingly (i.e. as clearly as possible) if it is to gain the attention it deserves and be understood.

✓ The editor must include items required by law but, to make it interesting, should consider adding a variety of additional information, presented in a way that can be easily comprehended by the target audience.

✓ Careful consideration needs to be given to the content of the Chairman's statement ensuring that items included in previous statements are not contradicted without explanation etc.

✓ The preparation of a summary financial statement and/or an employee report etc. may aid comprehension of the results by the target audiences.

chapter fourteen

No such thing
as bad publicity?

The public image

Who do we serve?

The requirements placed upon Boards are such that it may be all too easy for Directors concerned to look after the interests of shareholders, employees, the environment and the safety of visitors and yet overlook the fact that at the end of the day their companies can only survive if they remember to satisfy their customers – a party whose interests it is interesting to note are recognised in the consultative document that has started the process leading to a new companies act.

Impossible delegation

A customer was experiencing a series of problems with an account with one of the UK's largest banks and was so disillusioned with their performance that he wrote to the Managing Director. Back came a letter from the 'Manager, Customer Relations' who began her letter 'I have been asked to reply as we have overall responsibility in this department for the level of service provided by the Bank.'

What arrant nonsense – the only people who have **responsibility** for the level of service provided for their customers are the Board of Directors – and such responsibility can be delegated only at the peril of the business of the company. Such an attitude may explain why the financial services sector in general, and traditional banks in particular, are so poorly regarded by their customers.

Wealth-creating companies exist for one purpose only – to make a profit – an aim they can only achieve if they please and constantly please their customers. The company that fails its customers will ultimately fail itself. One of the top priorities for all Directors is therefore ensuring the satisfaction of their customers – and more of them.

A customer's perception of a company is derived from a number of sources – personal experience, quality of product and/or service, estimates of value for money, and, increasingly the perception of others notably those in the media. For the

Board, hand-in-hand with the responsibility to their customers must go the responsibility for the protection and preservation of company product, name and reputation. The operations and activities of organisations (particularly those which have a high consumer profile) and the individuals that control or direct them are increasingly subject to the attention of 'the media' and through them the public. The range of such interest – like the scope of the laws that govern companies and their operations – seems ever-increasing. Indeed it is the development of the laws and a company's compliance (or more likely non-compliance) with them which tend to generate much of this media interest. For example, the extension of employment law in recent years has led directly to media interest in, and scrutiny of Employment Tribunal hearings of occurrences and disputes which would formerly have been regarded as purely internal matters, not warranting any interest from third parties. Thus the interface with the public, and the continuing effect on the public perception of the company can alter on a daily basis. Without awareness and control, a positive image can be converted to the opposite very swiftly – with potentially disastrous effect on customers, demand and thus the business.

A protection policy

Reputation and public awareness may be indefinable and incapable of quantification, nevertheless their value can be considerable. A reputation can take years to build – and just seconds to lose – as witness the events following Gerald Ratner's presentation to the Institute of Directors when, following him comparing to 'crap' some of the products sold by his company's shops, the company bearing his name almost failed, its name had to be changed and 200 shops had to be sold. In addition, Ratner's own career was rudely interrupted as he was forced to resign firstly as Chairman of the company and then as a Director. Protecting the reputation of the company from all-comers should be high on the list of priorities of every Board. But what is required is a proactive rather than reactive approach. A suitable policy/procedure should be adopted.

Public relations commitment

- The company recognises the natural interest that will be evinced by the media on behalf of the public as well as the public itself in its operations and will make all information, other than that which is regarded as confidential, regularly available primarily to accredited sources

  Note: Such sources would include named journalists, a list of journals, newsletters, radio and TV outlets (as well as any Internet Web site) etc., and be included on a mailing list of those who would automatically be sent all literature produced for external use as a matter of course. In this way dependable information would be available to such sources which may result in facts being substituted for supposition which may be used if such information is not available.

- [Name and deputy] will act as company spokesperson and will be briefed continually by [Directors/executives as applicable] responsible for each [division, product, etc.]

- In the event of other employees being contacted by representatives of the media, they will be referred to the spokesperson

- In interfacing with the media, the spokesperson will endeavour to be truthful at all times, and to ensure that all information is correctly presented and correctly reported – endeavouring to correct the record where this is not the case

- Contacts with each branch of the media will be made and such contacts will be regularly briefed so that they have background knowledge of the organisation, which is then updated continuously

- In the event of a serious occurrence the senior manager responsible must brief the spokesperson as quickly as possible

- On no occasion regardless of the circumstances should the products, services or reputation of the organisation or of any person working in it or of any third party connected with it be called into doubt or questioned in any way whatever without the knowledge of [name].

Devising and using media releases

Capturing the attention

From time to time (and only when there is a real piece of news to impart) a media release can be issued. The media receive such a mass of information that only the most newsworthy will capture their attention. Strict parameters should be observed.

Media release

1. The subject matter must be really newsworthy – not to the organisation but to the target readers/listeners/ viewers of the media targeted.

2. Newsworthy subject matter must be made attention-worthy. Thus the release should both capture initial attention and provide all the relevant information in an easy to read (and use) form. If the first paragraph does not grab the reader's attention, no matter how good the rest of the document, it is unlikely to be read.

   Further, if the release is written in a way whereby the editor can use it (or more likely a part of it) without much editing, re-writing or recourse to the contact named (see below) then it stands a better chance of being used.

3. The release should be as brief as possible commensurate with the subject matter. Further, the language used should be simple, straightforward and should avoid jargon. Trying to 'pad out' a short release with extraneous information may mean the whole thing is discarded.

4. A release is not the place to build a climax. The most important point should be featured first or prominently. Everything else should support or explain this 'headline' material.

5. A release is not the correct conduit for organisation promotion – if attempted, it will fail. The purpose of a release is to provide information that it is believed will be of interest to the readers/listeners/viewers as a news item – not as promotional puff.

6. A quote from the Managing Director, or better still from a household name customer or equivalent will add interest.

7. If the release features a product and it is feasible to do so, include a sample with it. As a (poor) substitute, a photograph might be used. If a number of photographs are available, reference to this in the release and a crib of what is available might generate interest providing obtaining the photo is made easy and in a form capable of being used by the editor.

   Note: If samples are sent, the greatest care should be taken to send the best quality items.

8. If providing advance information about a forthcoming event ensure that the information is 'in advance'. Giving less than a week's notification is unlikely to generate any interest.

9. Keep a careful note of the correct names, positions and addresses of all those on the mailing lists – and keep all the details updated. Addressing releases to the wrong person, or the right person with the wrong title, or to either at the wrong address, reflects poorly on the organisation.

10. Always incorporate a contact name and telephone number and ensure that the contact is available on that number at the times stated after the release has been issued.

Golden rules – the four 'ONLYs'

1. Only issue a release when something of interest to the target audience is to be featured.

2. Only issue a release if it passes the 'blind man's test'. This comprises reading the release once only to someone who knows nothing of the subject matter and will have no chance to re-read it and asking them to state the story. Unless they can repeat the salient facts the release needs to be re-written – and probably shortened.

3. Only issue a release to the particular part of the media who are likely to be interested in the item.

4. Only issue the release if there is someone always on call ready and prepared to answer questions and provide additional data should the target media channel require this.

Media interviews

The policy statement on page 268 covers the area of media/public interest in very general terms and needs developing to address individual circumstances. As far as the spokesperson is concerned however they will need to have access to a range of data and to be in command of the latest developments at all times. No media briefing or interview will be successful unless adequate preparation and research has been carried out. Thus the items set out in the checklist below, need to be addressed. Inevitably the media will often try to obtain statements or comments from the Chairman or Chief Executive. Unless such persons have received training in communicating with the media, it may be preferable for a more junior but trained or experienced person to act as spokesman. Good Chairman do not always make good spokespersons. Whoever is chosen, they must be able to keep calm under pressure, to think swiftly, to appreciate that some answers may be double-edged (i.e. that either response may be self-critical) and to try to avoid this effect, and, above all to show their knowledge is sound.

Interviews

General research

- Identify the areas of operation in which the media/ public could be interested

- Identify the target audiences and the information they will require

- Identify the nature of the interest of each target audience and what information will be required

- Establish who is to deal with the ongoing enquiry and how they are to be briefed and updated concerning progress and all related aspects

- Encourage the spokesperson to create links with representatives of all media (establishing names, positions, main interests or 'angles', deadlines, potential bias etc.)

- Regularly examine stories and reports concerning the company to ensure the (correct/required/ positive) image is being created

- Continually develop questions (and, more importantly, answers thereto) that the company least wants asked and become conversant with both (updated as necessary)

- Prepare and update a résumé of all the recent successes of the company so that good news is available which may leaven the bad.

Particular preparation

- Before agreeing to the interview discover as much as possible about the circumstances (name of interviewer, programme, general purpose, scope of enquiry, whether live or recorded, scope for restricting/controlling questions, length of item to be used and likely use date, etc.)

- As comprehensive and complete brief as possible must be prepared on the subject matter and supporting items – company data, performance, products, problems, plans, etc.

- If the topic is likely to be controversial or embarrassing, appropriate responses and statements should be prepared, ideally trying to limit the 'damage' that could be caused or to develop news which offsets the effect

- The spokesperson needs to have total control of the brief, of all facts and of prepared responses, to be able to speak knowledgeably concerning the subject matter. Any hesitation, lack of confidence or inadequate knowledge will be communicated to the listener or viewer and create doubt and/or undermine veracity. In this respect it may be better to admit 'I don't know' rather than trying to 'flannel' through an answer. At least saying 'I don't know' (although it should only be used once or twice in any one interview) does have the ring of truth about it and can indicate – and win plaudits for – honesty and straightforwardness

- Three or four simple messages, or arguments that the company wishes to promote, must be developed, possibly with 'changes of direction' sentences, so that if the interviewer leads off in one direction, the spokesperson may be able to direct it to the company's preferred message. This approach needs to be controlled since a constant refusal to answer the actual questions put may lead to a more inquisitive or confrontational interview

- There should be no assumption that the interviewer will not have full knowledge of all the facts. It is better to assume that everything is known and then prepare answers accordingly

- The spokesperson must be ready for the 'off the cuff' and unrehearsed question deliberately introduced and designed to catch him/her unawares leading to the making of an unprepared or unwise comment or answer

- The spokesperson must be able to keep calm under pressure and/or goading, to be able to think quickly and laterally in order to fend off or turn aggression and criticism, to retain control, and, above all, NEVER lose their temper

- Most live media interviews last a minute or less and thus it may be possible only to put across two or three authoritative comments. The spokesperson needs to be calm, alert and interested and serious – never humorous, flustered, or flippant. To a large extent, particularly on television, the manner a message is delivered can be more effective than the content

- They should take a little time to think about the questions – asking for them to be repeated if necessary

- False statements should not be allowed to pass unchecked – the record should be corrected, tactfully but firmly

- Be positive not defensive. It may be better to 'own up' to a bad performance or event with a 'promise to improve' or rectify, rather than trying to defend an untenable position. The latter alternative will normally display the company in a poor light regardless of the circumstances – the impression will be 'they have learned nothing from the mistake', so nothing will change. This is particularly important when there has been loss, injury or death. In such instances it is essential that genuine sympathy is expressed and that there is an indication that steps are being taken to try to ensure there is no repetition.

During an interview concerned with bad news, particularly if it reflects poorly on the company, some rapport with, or positive feeling from, the audience may be gained if the spokesperson can, provided the circumstances are suitable, introduce details of facts that show the company in a better light – or at least try to put the current incident in some kind of perspective.

Communication aspects of crisis reaction

Whilst briefing the media on the more mundane aspects of company performance may be relatively easy, dealing with such interest in the aftermath of a calamity or disaster, poses considerable problems capable of being tackled only if based on contingency planning, i.e. anticipating the disaster and making advance plans for dealing with the effects. The advantage of 'planning for disaster' is that lengthy and calm thought can be given to alternative tactics and reactions, without the considerable time pressure for reaction that the incidence of disaster can cause. In addition, consideration of alternative actions in the event of disaster, may suggest beneficial changes in current operations. Obviously, if it is to be of value, such planning must be both comprehensive and regularly updated. Accordingly it will be an expensive operation, albeit one that should be regarded as an investment – certainly trying to cope with the innumerable requirements for action and comments following a disaster without at least a little planning will be virtually impossible.

Increasingly, as a means of determining appropriate cover for insurance purposes insurers are encouraged to consider first a process of risk management. Many of the 'disasters' that could generate media interest would be included in the process of risk management and linking these twin approaches could be beneficial. In any event, included in any 'insurance generated' disaster plan should be consideration of the requirement to deal with the media.

Crisis communication

1. Initial contact will usually be by telephone. A person should be nominated (possibly the Company Secretary, though there should always be one or two back up personnel) to handle all initial queries.

2. Listen carefully to what the enquirer is asking.

3. Make notes of (or tape record) the call content, time, the caller's name, position and media represented, the caller's telephone number and location.

4. Do not respond to questions, comments, observations – simply make notes as set out above and state that by a (specified) time someone will respond either in a news release or by telephone, e-mail, etc.

5. Do not be flustered by indications of deadlines. Those are the caller's problems not yours. Attempted insistence on immediate response, outrageous accusations, innuendoes etc. should also be noted but not commented upon.

6. By the time promised (not less than an hour) ensure someone does ring the caller back with comments.

7. Keep responses, press statements etc., short. Embroidery can both offset the punch effect and provide angles from which the reporter can come back at the author.

8. Provide a contact name/number.

9. Should such contact be used – the above guidelines should be applied – if necessary with the spokesperson ringing back after time for thought.

Event impact

When Harold Macmillan was Prime Minister and the Conservative Party was riding high, someone commented that it was difficult to see what could impact their position – 'Events, dear boy, just events' Macmillan is reported to have replied. Despite all the planning and preparation in the world, reputation and prospects can be damaged by events over which the company may feel it has little control. This is reality – even if unfair! The ramifications of employment law are such that many employers need to appear in an Employment Tribunal to defend their actions. Such is the complexity of the law that even organisations which are correctly regarded as 'models of good employment principles and practice' have needed to defend tribunal actions and several have lost such cases. The problem for the employer is that the fact of appearing can be taken as adverse by many employees whilst the circumstances of the case, since the vast majority of such cases are open to the public and many are reported in the local and national media, are available for all to review and consider.

Hypocritical?

a) A leading company known for its positive and progressive employment practices was found to have unfairly dismissed an employee who was injured (and eventually unable to resume her normal job) whilst trying to protect her employer's goods from a thief.

b) A company refused to pay Statutory Sick Pay to an employee who injured her back whilst working for them. Their point was that she was employed on a daily contract and thus did not accrue the three months service necessary to enable her to claim SSP. The Court of Appeal held her eight months service on single day contracts was 'continuous' and thus she was entitled to be paid.

c) An employer refused to allow a woman the holiday to which she was entitled because it had accrued during the time she was on maternity leave. The legislation states that a woman is entitled to all 'non-monetary' benefits at such a time. Her claim was upheld.

The exact circumstances of these cases will not concern most of those who will read or hear about the decisions at the time as they will tend to judge on the effect as reported rather than the reasons. What is important is that in each case the employer could be regarded by many as 'doing the wrong thing' which sends messages to all onlookers – not least the other employees in the company without whose efforts the Board will be unable to achieve its aims. It would be hardly surprising if the reaction to such cases was negative, and as a result, morale and commitment to the companies were impaired. Were these the kind of messages the organisations wished to send not just to their employees but also to all others doing business with them? If not, should not the Board have been able to avoid the messages being conveyed?

....

Make the decision

It may of course be that there were precedents which needed to be protected, or principles to be maintained which led to the above cases being fought. If so, and the decisions were taken at the top of each organisation then hopefully the effect of losing was taken into account and the cases were thought to be worth the cost of resisting if not, then perhaps, like the bank in the case study on page 266, responsibility has been delegated too far. In the generation of such messages, the Board needs to be in control, be seen to be in control and to be adopting the positions that it wants, not as may be suspected here, defending positions foisted upon them by more junior managers. Although it has been stated that there is no such thing as bad publicity, the Board will never know whether it lost sales as a result of some onlookers feeling dissatisfied at the company's approach.

Of course it is not only in the field of employee relations that such 'messages' can be publicised. A company which has a reputation for not paying its accounts promptly, or for always dealing harshly with those with whom it does business (whether buying or selling), or which refuses to support local charitable activities can swiftly build a reputation at variance to, but possibly more accurate than, that it which it may strive to give. It may be preferable to adopt as policy:

'All decisions which may result in legal action and/or generate publicity and public attention should only be taken

   a) At a senior level in the organisation [by name/ position], and

   b) After a full assessment has been made of the financial effect of the decision, the precedent involved and the effect of the result of the action on both internal and external audiences.

Failure to retain such control to the Board and/or to require that everyone seeks to maintain reputation or adheres to corporate style may lead to a situation where employees who need to represent the organisation – or give or interpret its rules externally have to operate by devising their own guidelines and style guide. This can only lead to inconsistencies and mean that decisions related to the appearance and promotion of the entity are not being taken in a cohesive and considered way, but rather executed in a piecemeal and fragmented manner not at all reflective of the way the company sees itself and wishes others to see it.

Corporate style/approach guidelines

1. The organisation as a responsible operator and employers will endeavour to communicate to all interested parties those details regarding its activities which may be of interest to them.

2. The areas of information that will be constantly reported upon are – future plans, new products (once any confidential aspects are removed), competitive position, details regarding employment and benefits and social responsibility programme.

3. Information will be provided usually in written form under the authority of a [Director] to ensure compliance with these guidelines.

4. This company has developed a reputation for [honest dealing, good value products, quality service and responsible employment] over the years and wishes these characteristics to guide all connected with it in their work and their relationships with external audiences at all times. No exceptions to these guidelines are acceptable. Failure to adhere to these precepts will be regarded very seriously.

5. Interviews can be granted with advance notice and an indication of the range of topics likely to be covered. Those interviewed will be required to comment only on items indicated in advance as being the subject matter. If questions outside this area are posed, the spokesperson will be required to answer 'policy requires that I do not answer questions on those subjects since I have not been briefed upon them'. Directors asked such questions may comment in general terms without committing the organisation.

6. All newsworthy information about the organisation will be published in media releases and in all cases a contact will be provided so that additional information can be obtained.

Summary checklist

✓ Retain responsibility for dealing with customers and customer care in widest sense of word to the Board so that those who have the ultimate responsibility know at first hand the opinions and attitudes of customers.

✓ Devise and adhere to a public relations policy and brief those required to interface with the media.

✓ Issue media releases only when subject is really newsworthy to those not otherwise involved with the company.

✓ Coach and brief all those required to give interviews and research reason for interview before agreeing to participate.

✓ Be prepared to provide infornation to media following a crisis and reflect this need in all disaster planning.

✓ Control events likely to generate attention directed in public arena resulting in adverse comment and potential reputation damage.

chapter fifteen

Into the new millennium

Corporate governance in the 21st century

The scope of anticipated changes

The scope of anticipated changes

It is fitting, as the 20th century draws to a close, that consultation should take place regarding a new format of Company Law which will have considerable impact on Directors and the governance of companies. Ironically the fact that time, an entirely man-made device, indicates that the century has changed, should not really have any effect. Realistically, however, the start of a new millennium, like the start of a new year, does encourage the contemplation of change. Humans, however, are creatures of habit, and thus it would not be surprising if this created a dichotomy between millennium-prompted reformers and reactionaries.

Regardless of any such antipathy however, it is inevitable that change will occur – and also that the rate of change will increase. Being ultimately responsible to their shareholders for the preservation, protection and growth of the company, Directors must be ready to face – even embrace – these changes. Areas where quite fundamental changes can be expected include:

- Liability
- Veracity
- Creativity
- Transparency
- Accountability
- Flexibility and
- Jollity.

In addition, and as an even more major requirement, Boards will need to develop a new relationship with employees and others working for their organisations.

Liability

Reference has been made throughout this book to the increasing liabilities placed on those that direct organisations. The extent and severity of such liabilities seems destined to continue to grow. Within the next 18 months in the UK the Law Commission is expected to finalise its proposals to strengthen the law (and penalties) against employers who bring about the deaths of, or cause injuries to, their employees and/or others. The current proposals are that three categories of offence would be created:

- 'Reckless killing': which would result from a person's unreasonable and conscious (even calculated) decision to run the risk of causing death or serious injury;

- 'Killing by gross carelessness': which would result from a person's conduct being below the level that should be expected and runs the obvious risk of death or serious injury; and

- 'Corporate killing': which would allow the prosecution of a company where its conduct falls below that which should be reasonably expected since it would then be in breach of its obligation to provide a safe system and place of work.

The fines that could be levied are unlimited and compensation could also be ordered to be paid to the families of victims.

Note: In the USA it is increasingly common for executives to take out their own indemnity insurance – often of sums of $2,000,000 or more. Given the trend towards more personal liability those in charge of companies might wish to consider emulating this practice although the rule that one cannot insure for the effects of an illegal act will still apply.

Veracity

Mainly because of well-publicised scandals and a widespread perception or suspicion that the prime task of those at the top of many of the UK's companies seems to be to feather their own nests, the regard with many of those in control are held by society in general is at a pretty low ebb. Increasingly it is likely that what will be demanded is more akin to partnerships with suppliers (as is already the case with several leading companies), employees (see below) and even customers. These developments can only occur if there is a firmer belief and confidence in the integrity of those at the top. Unfortunately business life abounds with lies such as the following:

- 'The cheque is in the post' (both UK and EU legislation is awaited that will tighten the obligation to pay promptly and to declare the company's policy in this regard)

- 'The customer is king' (in which case why does research indicate that most top management places little priority on communicating with or satisfying existing customers yet considerable importance on attaining new business. Since it is five times as expensive to source a new customer than to retain an old one, it would appear some Boards have odd priorities and an even less understandable appreciation of economics)

- 'Our staff are our most valuable asset' (which is certainly the case although few companies seem to treat their employees in the way that one would think the 'most valuable asset' would be treated – see below)

- 'We create value for our shareholders' (which may sit oddly with some records which show that in years when performance is poor, and/or employees pay increases are restricted or numbers are reduced by redundancy, directoral rewards have been high).

If Directors and Boards are to gain a valued reputation and regain integrity with suppliers, customers, employees and shareholders such corporate lies (and any others) need to be outlawed.

Creativity

Where do most Directors originate? The answer is from the ranks of senior managers. However, the challenge of the position of director is vastly different from the function of a manager. Managers have a range of duties – usually within a pre-determined area of operation. Such duties tend to be clear cut and often with definite levels of performance as criteria. This is not true of Directors. The scope of their operation is not simply over the whole company irrespective of functional responsibilities, they also have the major task of driving the company forward, of planning for the future, of creating the products or services that will be in demand – not next month, but next year and in five years time. To do this requires:

- A creative approach

- An ability to spend time in thought in preference to action, and

- Being able to prioritise and to marshal the various assets at their command.

One could almost summarise their respective responsibilities as (for managers) the ability to deal with pre-determined issues in a hands on manner (after all the origin of the word 'manager' is the Latin 'manus' = hand), and (for Directors) the ability to 'dream' (or at least think without limitation) and innovate.

Few Directors state that they have time to think, create and plan in such a fashion and yet such an approach is essential if the company is not to stagnate. The products and services we market and sell today are the result of long since past initiatives, hopefully in the more recent past we have initiated products for tomorrow. The successful Board is one that is already considering and designing the products or services that they believe will be wanted by the consumer of next year or the next decade. To quote Peter Drucker 'the enterprise that does not innovate inevitably ages and declines and in a period of rapid change such as the present, an entrepreneurial period, the decline will be fast'. As already noted the rate of change is likely to increase still further in the 21st Century – placing more pressure on Boards to invest in creativity and flexible responses.

'Tis better to have tried and lost than never to have tried'

Boards are appointed by shareholders not simply to guard the existing assets but also to take the business forward bearing in mind that companies do not stand still – they either expand and survive or contract and ultimately go out of business. Richard Branson was identified as one businessman in whom supervisors, surveyed in over 100 recent seminars throughout the UK, had confidence as both Director and leader. Reflecting his entrepreneurial style, his company Virgin has invested in several ventures far removed from the original record label which was the foundation of his fortune. In some instances the gambit has not been successful and the response has been to criticise – even ridicule – the idea. This reaction is nonsensical. It may be unfortunate that the idea did not work but the important factor as far as the corporate body is concerned is that the new venture was tried. Attempting to diversify may be risky – but sticking only with what is tried and tested can only ultimately lead to the demise of the company. The challenge for Directors is to learn from failure and to use the experience gained in future endeavours.

The Egyptian pyramid

Perhaps directors should visualise themselves sitting on top of a pyramid which represents their company. They may be tempted to regard the lines of the pyramid and its bulk and to take pride in its existence. It might be better to raise their eyes and look around – not least at the atmosphere which ultimately will destroy the structure. Boards must look outwards not inwards. Companies do not exist as islands immune from their environment – and sometimes the environment can destroy the company. The number of household name companies – some market leaders – that no longer exist is legion. Perhaps their Boards were too busy admiring the sides of the pyramid.

(Those with their eyes firmly focussed internally might also like to consider that the top of the pyramid only remains in place because of its base and what lies between the two.)

Transparency

In terms of corporate governance, at least as far as listed PLCs are concerned, change is endemic and already taking place, not least due to the recommendations of the Cadbury, Greenbury and Hampel committees already referred to. The inception and deliberations of these committees reflected widespread concerns (replicated in countries such as the USA, Japan, France, Germany, Australia etc.) regarding control of and the increasing power of corporate bodies – particularly resulting from the globalisation of markets and businesses. Already there are corporations that are wealthier than some Third World countries and with the incidence of international mergers there exists an imminent prospect of the creation of a few mega-corporations rivalling the size, power and influence of larger countries. Politicians in western democracies are, at least in theory, subject to control by the ballot box. No such control exists over corporations, the Boards of which can be largely self-perpetuating.

It is partly for this reason that in recent years that there have been several initiatives aimed at encouraging those who own companies to become more aware of the activities of those who direct them and to provide or exercise guidance and controls over them. The Department of Trade & Industry has published a number of consultation documents concerning shareholder reporting and interfacing and a number of institutional shareholders have gone on record requiring actions (e.g. restricting the length of service contracts to one or two years) aimed at curbing the opportunity for boards or individual members to abuse their powers.

These initiatives have so far been aimed at PLCs, but there is an inevitable overspill into the whole corporate arena. Basically what PLCs are required to do today, may well be required of all companies tomorrow. Generally Directors need to anticipate being required to provide greater and more detailed explanations of activities, strategies and attitudes.

In its 1998 survey of professional development issues the Institute of Directors commented that a Director must be able:

- To think strategically

- To provide his company with vision

- To stand back from the everyday problems and look at the company's situation today and tomorrow

- To provide leadership and

- To communicate strategy and vision to all employees.

This is broadly the same list of aims that is set out in the Institute's own 'Standards for the Board'.

Accountability

Currently Company Law requires Directors to produce each year a report of their company's activities – the Annual Report. As previously noted most of these are couched in language, format and presentation that neither entices the reader to study them, nor provides information in a readily accessible fashion. A 1998 survey of over 100 leading companies indicated that although 75 per cent of those asked felt the Annual Report was an important way of communicating with the target audiences, 60 per cent actually produced it only with the 'City of London audience' in mind. This can hardly be said to be evidence of a genuine wish to report meaningfully with those who own the company let alone with other interested parties.

The 1990s recession left many consumers far more aware of price and value, more conservative about their expenditure – and demanding acceptable levels of delivery, service, and quality. Retail demand in the UK is not expected to regain the level it reached at the height of its boom in the middle 1980s until the first few years of the 21st century (and the current downturn is likely to further delay regaining that level), whilst many producers of goods and providers of services are being forced to operate in markets, smaller than hitherto and unlikely to grow rapidly – if at all. Demand is thus under pressure and customer retention rather than new customer acquisition is key. P Four (a marketing consultancy) carried out a survey in 1997 and discovered that although 70 per cent of the top management representatives who were asked felt that customer focus was a first or second priority, less than 25 per cent felt that time spent with customers was important. Far too many Boards are remote from customers (on whom they depend for the continuation for their business) and display what can be termed corporate arrogance to both customers and shareholders (and probably their employees). Both categories (as well as employees) are likely to be far more demanding and vocal in the 21st century.

Whilst not ideal for the purpose, the Annual Report provides an opportunity to 'market' the company and its products or services in an advantageous light – yet only 30 per cent of those in the above survey saw the report as serving this need. The document is required to be produced in any event – why not make it work and use it to market the organisation to all with whom it interfaces? Perhaps in the new century the trend will become what a few companies already do which is to produce two reports – one concentrating on financial aspects and one which endeavours to provide a meaningful commentary. Unlike the present reports however perhaps we should redesign the latter so that they concentrate on where the company is going and the means by which it reaches its target. Such a document could put flesh on the bare bones of the figures and in addition it might allow Boards to demonstrate the way ahead rather than, as is done in current Annual Reports, focussing on what is past.

Increasingly more of the target audience will want to know:

- What the company stands for (in terms of ethics, environmental matters etc.)

- How it wishes to trade (attitudes on safety, value, quality etc.)

- How it interacts (i.e. with society as a whole as well as with suppliers, customers, employees, shareholders etc.)

and so on.

Companies that fail to address this need may find they lose their cutting edge. This is not meant to imply that the Annual Report can provide all the answers – a comprehensive programme of information provision is necessary. The first essential of such a programme is a willingness to commit to the principle of openness of information provision in which regard an informative user-friendly Report may be indicative of such commitment. Using modern technology (e.g. the internet) to disseminate information may be helpful.

It is vital that Boards should consider how they are to comply with the ever-increasing requirements of legislation. Whilst this may be delegated to the Company Secretary, it may require there to be a greater allocation of resources to this function so that directors can ensure that their companies are compliant. Any resistance to committing scarce resources to such a non-productive endeavour might best be answered by the provision of an analysis of current and potential exposures to personal liability. Such additional resources in the compliance area may then be seen to be a valuable (even essential) investment.

Flexibility

Change challenges what is known and trusted, forcing us to deal with what is new, unknown, and perhaps risky. The temptation may be to avoid the latter and stick with the former. However, Directors are paid to drive the company forward which must entail a willingness to embrace the new and the risky. Indeed it could be said that Directors are paid (and usually paid highly) in part to take risks (albeit having first analysed the opportunities and the dangers fully) since only if they do are the rewards for the company likely to be high. Legal changes are often unwelcome, and whilst such a reaction may be understandable, those who persist in 'opposing' the trend may do their companies a disservice. Such changes cannot be resisted and it might be more beneficial (and economic) to accept the new requirements and to assess whether there are any ways in which the company can use them to its own advantage.

Costly ignorance

A solicitor employed a number of staff and in addition advised some clients on Employment Law (which tempts an assumption that he must have known and understood its ramifications). However, within his own organisation not only were all the requirements of Employment Law totally ignored, it seemed that this was due not to oversight but to a conscious decision not to abide by the requirements.

At a tribunal brought by an employee who had been dismissed, questions regarding the provision of contracts, disciplinary procedures, equal opportunity policies etc. and even the proceedings themselves were treated by the employer with disdain – even arrogance. The tribunal found in favour of the employee and awarded her several thousand pounds compensation.

Key technique

a) Everyone is entitled to their own opinion of the law and many will feel, perhaps rightly, that some aspects of employment protection are excessive. Nevertheless the law is the law, ignorance is no excuse and non-compliance can be costly.

b) Disdain for tribunal proceedings may be a personal right – but it will hardly win friends and influence people.

Directors can be excused for antipathy towards legislation – and railing against it with the lawmakers may assist changes being made – but refusing to work within it is immature, foolish and costly as well as being a breach of the duty they owe to their shareholders. We are likely to see as the 21st century progresses, the 'sexual glass ceiling' shattered as more and more women occupy more and more senior positions. Once again this development will require fresh approaches not least in the area of personal and employment relationships (see below).

Jollity

We spend nearly a half of our waking life at work. Work has become for many a social activity even though it is also an economic necessity. A majority of lasting friendships, partnerships and even marriages are formed through workplace encounters. Indeed, so important a part of time can the working environment become that let alone financial consideration many are unable to cope with redundancy simply because as well as the stigma of 'not being wanted' they have to face the loss of the social interaction that working provides. (This is a very important consideration that those that implement redundancies often entirely overlook.) Since the workplace is where a considerable amount of time is spent, ideally the environment should be as convivial as possible. Perhaps 'jollity' pushes the point too far but many well-regarded leaders endeavour to create situations where at least work is enjoyable. An environment that is enjoyable is likely to be one in which employees can be motivated to produce their best work, to work together as a team and be encouraged to make suggestions for the improvement of existing and development of new products or services. It is likely that costly labour turnover can be reduced (retention of quality staff being currently recognised by many leading organisations as of vital importance) – whilst the reputation of such an employer creating such a environment may aid the recruitment of the 'best' people. That this should be so can be argued by considering the opposite type of environment. Employers known or regarded as 'poor' will find considerable difficulty recruiting decent calibre personnel.

Relationships

Inherent in the duties of a Director is the requirement to interface with a variety of people – suppliers, customers, shareholders, regulatory authorities and last, and certainly not least, employees, only through whom can they achieve their companies' aims. As recently as 30 years ago the relationship between company and employee was very much master and servant. In the intervening years a whole panoply of employment laws have changed that relationship to one where increasingly it needs to be regarded as a partnership and one where each partner must realise that at times the other may have priorities outside the company.

The notion of the male breadwinner and the female bread-distributor is long-gone and in many cases both partners of such traditional family units (themselves subject to marked change) now work (which will itself ultimately lead to the breaking of the glass ceiling for female employees) – whether by choice or, perhaps more widely, by necessity. The effect of the requirement for the twin income unit has been a development of protections particularly for women in their childbearing role. In turn, however, there is now a widespread expectation from society that males will share family responsibilities and the employment environment is currently grappling with the need to provide opportunities for them to do so.

In addition to a number of these 'pure employment' issues (e.g. minimum wage requirements, working time restrictions, provision of paid holidays, provision of leave for family crises etc.) the UK is required to implement the European Convention on Human Rights which, *inter alia*, grants to everyone the right to be accorded respect for their private and family life. With the current thinking of the European Union it is difficult to envisage any change in this climate – at least for the next 15 years or so. Right or wrong – such a climate is here to stay – another example of the need for those in charge of companies to accept and work within the new requirements.

Given such circumstances, aided by:

- A widening of popular share ownership enabling many more people to acquire at least a little capital and to understand the need for investment and profits to create new jobs (or simply maintain the old ones)

- A growing awareness that the days of confrontation may actually have achieved relatively little in the long term (as management guru Peter Drucker said 'adversarial management is fine as long as you don't have to see or work with the bastards again')

- The current UK government being more pragmatic regarding industrial relations, and particularly

- The UK's membership of a 'socially committed' European Union

a re-assessment of the employment relationship seems warranted.

This should entail moving away from the confrontational attitudes evident in many industries over the past 30 years, and from the 'macho management' generated by the curbing of Union power and lower demand, and towards a realisation that a genuine partnership based on mutual respect and trust between capital and labour may be the only way in which an improved and sustainable level of productivity and profitability can be achieved. That this may be a considerable challenge for some managements is inevitable. The report *Impact of People Management Practices on Business Performance*, concludes 'The results suggest that if managers wish to influence the performance of their companies, the most important area they should emphasise is the management of people. This is ironic given that our research has also demonstrated that emphasis on human resource management is one of the most neglected areas of managerial practice within organisations.'

Moving towards an employment partnership is not simply 'a good idea' or the latest fad, it is based on economic reality and advantage. In a report *Benchmarking the Partnership Company* the Involvement and Participation Association concluded of a number of companies committed to partnership that 'partnership pays off – organisations have a better psychological contract, there is greater trust between employees and employers and **performance is higher**'.

Employers' challenge

The initiators of this new relationship must be Directors in which regard the report of the Hampel Committee on Corporate Governance provides guidance: 'Business prosperity cannot be commanded. People, teamwork, leadership, enterprise and skills are what really produce prosperity... an effective Board... should lead and control the company.' The report does not use the word 'management' – the operative term is the more positive and dynamic term 'leadership' whereby people are motivated to perform as a team and above themselves.

Note: In this regard it is perhaps worth stressing that there are two motivational forces:

a) The basic requirement to earn a living for self and dependents, and

b) The motivation to perform well which depends for its existence and cultivation on the environment and treatment experienced in the workplace.

Unfortunately in the UK the number of managers able to motivate their employees in the workplace is relatively few – over 66 per cent admitted in a recent survey by recruitment specialists Robert Half, that they possess only limited motivational skills. Research indicates that the majority of employees want good management/leadership and to be treated with fairness and respect; unfortunately it seems that only a minority actually receive either – but if partnership is required, leadership by one of the partners is essential. Indeed it is arguable that because management did not lead in the 1950s and 1960s, the vacuum was filled by trades unions, a situation which led directly to their growth of power and influence. If management perform properly – i.e. communicate and lead as is both their right and their responsibility – there will be less opportunity for others to fill this vacuum; a telling comment as we enter a period where there is likely to be pressure for increased Union recognition.

Private/personal life balance

The various protections and rights granted by employment legislation of recent years are leading to a situation where employers are being required to create an employment scenario which is 'family friendly'. Indeed there is already increasing pressure in this regard – not least from those aged 18-35 (whose views will increasingly become the norm). The concept that employees personal pressures and commitments are nothing to do with their employers is unlikely to remain a sustainable view in employment in the 21st century which even now increasingly it is not. Inevitably the best performers can pick and choose their employers, and employers that wish to obtain and retain the best employees will increasingly be those that accept the need for balance and provide assistance for their employees in coping with their personal obligations. The range of 'benefits' available to employees (of which a number are listed in the following checklist) has increased rapidly over the past decade and the rate of increase is likely to increase still further.

Employee benefits

- Flexible hours

- Increased time-off whether paid or unpaid

- Job sharing

- Annualised hours

- Homeworking

- Paternity and family leave

- 'Cafeteria' contracts (where the employee can select the range of benefits suitable to their situation at any time)

- Crèches for both children and elderly relatives being cared for

- Facilities for 'trailing spouses' (i.e. partners of those whose employer has required them to relocate possibly overseas)

  and so on.

The overriding requirement however is to treat employees with respect which requires those in charge of companies to listen to the views of their employees which is not only good practice but is also a legal requirement in many instances.

Effective consultation is, however, not achieved by compliance with legal requirements – it requires a genuine commitment from both partners. But companies that have tried this, report that rarely is there any employee resistance, in most cases it resembles pushing against an open door. A recent survey indicated that what employees want from their jobs is:

- 87 per cent – to be treated fairly

- 80 per cent – challenging work

- 77 per cent – to be able to get on with the job.

This is hardly evidence of an unwillingness to work or be involved. However, far fewer employees stated that they were satisfied with the fairness and respect that they received in their jobs. It is difficult to see how employers can maximise output from dissatisfied employees.

The sting in the tail?

The essential challenge for the 21st Century is for Directors to be able to respond (and respond swiftly) to changing demands of a fast changing society. This may be difficult for some to embrace. As Gary Hamel (co-author of *Competing for the Future*) stated recently 'Where are you likely to find people with least diversity of experience, the largest investment in the past and the greatest reverence for industry dogma? – At the top'. Yet it is from people at the top (and only from that source) that can come:

- The preparedness and willingness to face the challenges of tomorrow

- The ability to provide creativity, drive and vision

  and, above all

- Leadership (bearing in mind as Stephen Covey, an American leadership guru said recently, 'Management is about doing things right but leadership is doing the right things.')

Appendices

Case references

BMK Holdings Ltd *v* Logue
(1993 ICR 601 EAT)

Bryans *v* Northumberland College of Arts & Technology
(1995 People Management 10/95)

Buchan *v* Secretary of State for Employment
(1997 IRLR 80)

Denco *v* Joinson
(1991 ICR 172 EAT)

Dentmaster (UK) Ltd *v* Kent
(IDS 601, 11/97)

D'Jan of London Ltd (Copp *v* D'Jan)
(1BCLC 561 1994)

Dorchester Finance Co Ltd & anor. *v* Stebbing and ors
(1989 BLLC 498)

Enterprise Glass Co Ltd *v* Miles
(1990 EAT 538/89)

Fleming *v* Secretary of State for Trade & Industry
(1997 IRLR 682)

Heffer *v* Secretary of State for Trade and Industry
(25.9.96 EAT 355/96)

Hutchings *v* Coinseed
(Court of Appeal 1998 IRLR 190)

Ivey *v* Secretary of State for Employment
(1997 IRLR 80)

Jones *v* Tower Boot
(1997 ICR 254 CA)

McLean *v* Secretary of State for Employment
(1992 (S) EAT 672/91)

National Rivers Authority *v* Alfred
McAlpine Homes East Ltd

Secretary of State for Trade & Industry *v* Bottrill
(1998 IRLR 120)

William Hill Organisation Ltd *v* Tucker
(Court of Appeal 1998 IRLR 313)

Bibliography

Benchmarking the Partnership Company,
Birkbeck College and the London School of Economics,
Involvement and Participation Association

Chartered Secretary – monthly journal of the Institute of
Chartered Secretaries and Administrators
(ICSA Tel: 0171 580 4741)

*Company Law Reform – Modern Company Law for a
Competitive Economy* (DTI 1998 Tel: 0171 215 5000)

Financial Reporting to Employees – a practical guide,
David M Martin, Gee 1997 (Tel: 0171 393 7400)
David M Martin (Tel: 01992 572536)

*Committee on Corporate Governance (Hampel Final
Report)* Gee/Committee on Corporate Governance 1998
(Tel: 0171 393 7400)

*Impact of People Management Practices on Business
Performance*, Patterson, West, Lawthom and Nickell IPD
1998 (Tel: 0171 263 3434)

*Manipulating Meetings, Tough Talking, How to be a
Great Communicator*, David M Martin, Pitman/Institute
of Management 1996 (Tel: 0171 379 7383)

Making Corporate Reports Valuable, The Institute of
Chartered Accountants of Scotland, Kogan Page 1988

Making it happen, Sir John Harvey-Jones, Collins 1988

*One Stop Company Secretary, One Stop Personnel,
One Stop Communication, One Stop Customer Care*,
David M Martin, ICSA/Prentice Hall 1996
(Tel: 01442 881900)

Standards for the Board, Institute of Directors, 1995
(Tel: 0171 839 1233)

Summary Financial Statements – The way forward,
Professor R Hussey, a report by the Institute of Chartered
Accountants, Butterworths 1996 (Tel: 0117 965 6261)

Thorogood: the publishing business of the Hawksmere Group

Thorogood publishes a wide range of books, reports, special briefings, psychometric tests and videos. Listed below is a selection of key titles.

Other Desktop Guides

The company director's desktop guide
David Martin   £15.99

This book is essential reading for all directors and professional advisers and will ensure that the reader meets their legal responsibilities, anticipates and resolves problems and works effectively with all parts of the business. The principal areas which are addressed are directors' responsibilities: formal procedures and documents, leadership and management, corporate governance, working with shareholders and public aspects of directorship. Corporate governance in the 21st century is also addressed in this detailed guide.

The company secretary's desktop guide
Roger Mason   £15.99

This is a clear comprehensive guide to the complex procedures and legislation governing effective company legislation. All aspects of the Company Secretary's work is covered including share capital, share registration and dividends; accounts and auditors; mergers and acquisitions; profit sharing and share option schemes in addition to voluntary arrangements, administration orders and receivership. This fully up-to-date, practical guide is essential reading for Company Secretaries, Directors, Administrators, Solicitors and Accountants.

The credit controller's desktop guide
Roger Mason   £15.99

A comprehensive guide to collecting debts effectively, this book covers all aspects of the credit controller's work. Written in a clear, practical style, the author, who has considerable experience of credit control for over 20 years, includes case studies, standard letters and forms and an update on the latest legal developments. Key issues covered include credit control policies, legal action (principles to follow and how to achieve a satisfactory outcome through the courts), as well as factoring, credit agencies and credit insurance.

Masters in Management

Mastering business planning and strategy
Paul Elkin   £19.99

Mastering financial management · *Stephen Brookson* £19.99
Mastering leadership · *Michael Williams*   £19.99

Mastering negotiations · *Eric Evans*   £19.99
Mastering people management · *Mark Thomas*   £19.99
Mastering project management · *Cathy Lake*   £19.99
Mastering personal and interpersonal Skills
Peter Haddon   £19.99

Essential Guides

The essential guide to buying and selling
unquoted companies · *Ian Smith*   £25

The essential guide to business planning and
raising finance · *Naomi Langford-Wood & Brian Salter* £25

The essential business guide to the Internet
Naomi Langford-Wood & Brian Salter   £19.95

Business Action Pocketbooks
– *edited by David Irwin*

Building your business pocketbook   £10.99
Developing yourself and your staff pocketbook £10.99
Finance and profitability pocketbook   £10.99
Managing and employing people pocketbook   £10.99
Sales and marketing pocketbook   £10.99

Other titles

The John Adair handbook of management
and leadership · *Edited by Neil Thomas*   £19.95
The handbook of management fads · *Steve Morris*   £8.95

The inside track to successful management
Dr Gerald Kushel   £16.95

The pension trustee's handbook (2nd edition)
Robin Ellison   £25

Boost your company's profits · *Barrie Pearson*   £12.99

The art of headless chicken management
Elly Brewer and Mark Edwards   £6.99

Thorogood also has an extensive range of Reports and Special Briefings which are written specifically for professionals wanting expert information.

For a full listing of all Thorogood publications, or to order any title, please call Thorogood Customer Services on 0171 824 8257 or fax on 0171 730 4293.